Instagram Growth Mastery

Get Followers Fast Using Trends, Hashtags & AI Tools

By Joe Correa

Published by Live Stronger Faster

This book is for educational and informational purposes only. The author and publisher are not engaged in rendering legal, financial, or other professional advice. Readers should consult a qualified professional before making any financial decisions.

First Edition

www.ingramcontent.com/pod-product-compliance
Lightning Source LLC
LaVergne TN
LVHW022229200926
848481LV00006B/2190
9798295653407

Table of Contents

Introduction

The world of Instagram has evolved far beyond a simple photo-sharing app, transforming into one of the most powerful platforms on the planet for attention, influence, education, entertainment, and business. Yet even though the opportunity has grown bigger, getting noticed has never felt more challenging. Millions of creators are posting daily, thousands of businesses are competing for the same audiences, and the algorithm is constantly shifting. For most people, this creates frustration. They post content that gets no reach, watch their follower count stay frozen, and wonder why some creators explode while they stay invisible. But the truth is that Instagram growth in 2025 is no longer a guessing game. It is a system. It is a science. It is a predictable process built on understanding three pillars: how the algorithm decides what to show, how Reels dominate reach, and how AI tools give modern creators an unfair advantage. This book is your blueprint for mastering all three.

Everything about Instagram has changed—except for one fundamental truth: the platform still rewards content that keeps people watching. In past years, growth felt mysterious, and creators believed success depended on "luck" or "going viral." Today, the data is clear. Instagram shows your posts to the people most likely to engage, and if that engagement holds, the content spreads far beyond your followers. That means growth no longer belongs to people with large followings. It belongs to people who understand systems. When you know which formats Instagram pushes, how to maximize retention, how to catch attention in the first three seconds, and how to position each post for the Explore page, growth becomes consistent instead of random. By the end of this book, you will understand exactly why certain creators gain 10,000 followers in a week while others gain nothing for months, even when they work just as hard.

Unlike older platforms, Instagram shifts attention rapidly and rewards those who adapt quickly. Reels are the number one growth engine now, responsible for 70–90% of new follower reach. Short-form video has reshaped the landscape, giving small creators massive leverage—if they know how to use it. Mastering Reels is not about luck; it is about hooks, pacing, pattern interrupts, sound selection, trend timing, and storytelling that holds attention to the final second. It is about understanding when to post, how often to post, and how the algorithm distributes content in waves. It is about knowing which topics pull in your target audience and which ones push them away. It is about creating videos that do not need to be perfect—they just need to be optimized. Most people overthink content; successful creators optimize it. This book will teach you how to turn your ideas into high-performing videos without spending hours editing or guessing what will work.

What makes Instagram growth in 2025 completely different from all previous years is the rise of AI. Tools like ChatGPT, Claude, Midjourney, and advanced editing apps have democratized content creation. You no longer need professional skills in writing, design, scripting, or video editing. AI can generate hooks, scripts, captions, hashtags, content calendars, and even Reels ideas in seconds. It can rewrite your videos to retain viewers longer. It can repurpose your old posts into carousel scripts or story prompts. It can analyze competitors and reveal what you should post next. Creators who understand this have exploded on the platform. Those who ignore these tools fall behind. This book gives you the exact AI prompts, tools, templates, and methods used by creators who scale their accounts at lightning speed with half the time and effort. When you combine the algorithm's needs with AI-powered speed, growth becomes inevitable.

But growth on Instagram is not just about going viral. It's about creating a brand people trust, follow, and return to. This requires consistency—something most creators struggle with. Not because they lack discipline, but because they lack systems. Posting every day is hard when you don't know what to post, when you fear being repetitive, or when the editing process takes too long. This book introduces you to a system-driven approach that removes all friction from your week. You will learn how to batch content for seven days in one afternoon, how to build a content timing strategy that maximizes reach, how to document your daily life into easy content, and how to create a repeatable workflow so you never run out of ideas again. Growth is not about motivation; it's about structure. When you follow the right structure, consistency becomes automatic instead of exhausting.

Another major shift happening on Instagram is the rise of micro-creators. Accounts with fewer than 10,000 followers are now being prioritized because small creators build communities faster than large creators. Instagram's algorithm knows this, and it rewards creators who post consistently on niche topics, engage with their audience, use optimized hashtags, and follow trend timing. That means *you* have more opportunity than ever before. Whether you want to become a personal brand, grow a business, start a faceless page, or simply monetize your creativity, this is the best time in history to build an Instagram presence. You don't need perfect videos. You don't need expensive equipment. You don't need years of experience. You need the right strategy—and you're holding it in your hands.

This book gives you a complete breakdown of how to grow on Instagram even if you're starting from zero. You will learn how the algorithm works, how to position your content for maximum reach, how to use hashtags the right way, how to choose the best niche, how to create scroll-stopping hooks, how to use trend waves to your advantage, and how to post at the perfect time for amplification. You'll discover how to build an irresistible profile, attract followers who actually care about your content, and use AI to outperform creators who spend hours manually planning everything. You will also learn what *not* to do—common mistakes that slow growth, kill engagement, and push your content to the bottom of your audience's feeds. These small errors often make the difference between accounts that grow quickly and accounts that stay stuck for years.

As you move through this book and the rest of the series, you will see how each volume builds upon the last. Book 1 gives you the complete foundation: growth systems, Instagram's algorithm, Reels strategy, and AI tools. Book 2 will teach you how to create viral Reels using hooks, trends, transitions, and timing. Book 3 will reveal how to build faceless Instagram pages that earn passive income using AI content and automation. Book 4 will teach you the secrets of Instagram SEO, hashtags, and ranking on the Explore page. Each book unlocks a new level of skill, helping you grow faster, earn more, and build a scalable Instagram ecosystem that does not depend on chance. By starting with Book 1, you are preparing yourself for rapid growth, long-term monetization, and a deep understanding of Instagram's inner mechanics.

Instagram in 2025 is a place of unlimited opportunity, but only for those who understand how it truly works. The algorithm is not your enemy; it is your partner. AI tools are not shortcuts; they are accelerators. Trends are not distractions; they are growth multipliers. Once you understand how these forces work together, you will never look at Instagram the same way again. You will see growth everywhere—inside trending audio, inside niche demand, inside content gaps, inside comments from your audience, inside AI-generated scripts, and inside everyday moments that transform into storytelling gold. Everything around you becomes content. Everything becomes an asset. Everything becomes part of your growth system.

By the time you finish this introduction, you are not just reading a book. You are entering a new era of your creator journey—one where you grow with intention, create with confidence, and build a digital presence that attracts followers daily. Whether your goal is 10,000 followers, 100,000 followers, or a full-time income as a creator, you now have the roadmap. The tools. The shortcuts. The clarity. Nothing about Instagram growth will be left to chance. This book will give you the exact strategies used by the fastest-growing creators in the world, and all you need to do is apply them. The next chapter begins now, and so does your rise.

Chapter 1

Understanding the Instagram Algorithm

Instagram growth has never been random. Even though millions of creators believe that the algorithm is unpredictable, unstable, or impossible to understand, the truth is that Instagram has always followed a clear formula rooted in human behavior and measurable engagement patterns. Once you understand this formula, you stop posting blindly and start creating with precision. You begin to recognize why certain videos reach millions while others barely reach your followers. You see how the platform evaluates content before distributing it, and you understand why Instagram rewards some creators with rapid growth and holds others back. This first chapter will reveal the mechanics behind visibility, reach, discovery, and recommendation systems so you can grow steadily instead of relying on luck.

At its core, Instagram is a machine trained to show people what they are most likely to enjoy, watch, share, comment on, or return to. Every time you open the app, Instagram studies your behavior: what you tap, what you scroll past, what you rewatch, what you save, what you comment on, and which creators you follow. Because Instagram's goal is to keep users on the platform longer, it rewards content that generates strong engagement and quickly demotes content that fails to capture interest. Understanding these signals is essential because Instagram's algorithm doesn't pick favorites—it picks performers. This means your follower count does not determine your reach. A small page can outperform a large one if the content is more engaging. This is why new creators can grow quickly once they understand the algorithm's priorities.

Instagram evaluates content using three key performance indicators: **click-through rate**, **watch time and retention**, and **engagement depth**. Click-through rate refers to whether people decide to watch your content in the first place. For Reels, this means whether they paused instead of swiping past. For feed posts, it means whether they stopped scrolling. For carousels, it means whether they swiped to the next slide. If people don't stop, Instagram assumes the content lacks appeal. Retention measures how long they watch. If people stay until the end of your Reel, you're rewarded. If they leave quickly, Instagram assumes the video doesn't deliver. Engagement depth includes likes, comments, shares, saves, profile taps, and follows. Shares and saves are the strongest signals because they indicate value. When content scores well across these metrics, Instagram increases distribution.

Another important factor is the **viewer-to-follower conversion rate**—how many viewers become new followers after watching your Reels or posts. Instagram wants to recommend creators who retain audiences and attract new ones naturally. This is why educational content, inspirational content, and entertaining content often outperform random lifestyle posts. When your content consistently turns strangers into followers, Instagram sees that you are contributing to the platform's ecosystem. The platform will then push your videos to more viewers because your page helps Instagram keep users active and engaged.

To maximize reach, creators must understand the four discovery areas inside Instagram: **the Reels feed**, **the Explore page**, **the Suggested Posts feed**, and **search-based discovery**. The Reels feed gives you the highest chance of reaching non-followers because Instagram aggressively pushes short-form videos to new audiences. The Explore page is where Instagram places content with high engagement and strong relevance signals. Suggested Posts appear in the main feed between posts from people you follow, and these are algorithmically chosen based on your interests. Search-based discovery uses keywords in your captions, text overlays, and profile bio to match your content with what people search for. A creator who understands how to engineer content for all four areas can grow exponentially faster than a creator who relies on only one. One of the biggest growth advantages comes from creating content that aligns with Instagram's priority categories: **relatability**, **education**,

inspiration, **transformation**, and **entertainment**. Relatability creates connection. Education delivers value. Inspiration motivates. Transformation shows before-and-after journeys. Entertainment delivers dopamine. Posts that fall into one of these categories naturally generate high watch time and engagement, while random daily updates rarely perform well. The algorithm rewards content that evokes curiosity, emotion, or utility. This is why hooks—your opening line or your first visual frame—are essential. Instagram needs evidence within the first two seconds that your content is worth showing to thousands of new viewers.

Creators also need to understand the concept of **content waves**. Instagram does not distribute your content all at once. It tests your Reel on a small batch of people. If metrics are strong, it expands reach to a larger group, then another group after that. This is why some Reels get a sudden spike in views hours or days after posting. If you see spikes, you're entering a new wave of distribution. If your views stop increasing, the content likely failed to pass a retention or engagement threshold. Understanding these waves helps you avoid deleting videos prematurely and helps you measure performance accurately.

Another powerful growth driver is the **topic-to-audience match**. Instagram uses advanced recommendation systems to connect viewers with specific interests. If your content consistently revolves around one niche—fitness, travel, finance, fashion, cooking, parenting, real estate, motivation, or beauty—the algorithm can categorize your page easily. But if your content is all over the place, Instagram doesn't know who to recommend you to, so your reach becomes unstable. This chapter will show you how to choose your niche, narrow your messaging, and structure your content so each post trains the algorithm to find your ideal followers.

Hashtags play a supporting role, but they are not as important as people think. Their purpose is to categorize your content, not make it go viral. Using a mix of broad, medium, and niche hashtags helps Instagram understand what your content is about. However, hashtags alone do not guarantee reach. They are one layer of visibility. The real growth comes from content quality, retention, and engagement. This book will teach you a strategic hashtag method that boosts ranking opportunities without depending on overused tags.

Ultimately, Instagram rewards consistency—not frequency alone, but consistent quality and messaging. Posting daily does not matter if the content lacks clarity or value. Posting three high-quality Reels per week can outperform posting seven low-quality ones. When your content is consistent, Instagram learns your patterns, your topics, and your audience—and begins recommending your account more aggressively. Growth becomes faster and more predictable.

The true secret behind Instagram is simple: the algorithm follows the audience. If you understand human behavior—curiosity, emotion, relevance, and value—you understand the algorithm. The goal of this chapter is to empower you with the ability to reverse-engineer visibility so your growth becomes purposeful, measurable, and strategic. As you move through this book, you will master the exact steps to create Reels, Stories, and Posts that outperform competitors and attract thousands of followers who genuinely care about your message. Instagram is a machine, but growth is human. When you learn both sides, everything changes.

"The Creator Who Stayed Invisible"

When Maya started her Instagram page, she believed she was doing everything right. She posted daily, used thirty hashtags, followed trends, and even invested in a professional camera. Yet no matter what she did, her account felt invisible. Her Reels barely reached a few hundred views, her posts received little engagement, and her follower count seemed permanently stuck. She watched other creators blow past her, gaining thousands of followers overnight, and she couldn't understand what she was doing wrong. The harder she tried, the more discouraged she became. She assumed Instagram was saturated, impossible, unfair, or reserved only for people with connections or good luck. What she didn't know was that she was missing the hidden formula that determines who gets seen—and who doesn't.

One evening, frustrated, she sat scrolling through her feed and noticed something strange. A small creator with fewer followers than her had a Reel with over a million views. Another creator with low production quality had a video with thousands of comments. But Maya, with all her effort, couldn't break through. She started to question everything. Was it her niche? Her editing? Her ideas? She didn't realize that none of those were the core issue. The real problem was that she was creating content without understanding how Instagram evaluated it. She was posting based on instinct instead of strategy.

The turning point came when she discovered how Instagram actually works. She learned that the platform didn't care about follower count or posting frequency. It cared about something far more predictable: whether people paused, watched, engaged, shared, or followed. When she looked at her own content through this lens, everything suddenly made sense. Her videos didn't have strong hooks. Her retention was low. Her topics were broad and unfocused. Her captions didn't support keyword discovery. Her niche was unclear. Her content didn't evoke emotion or value. It wasn't bad—it simply wasn't optimized for the way Instagram recommends content.

Maya decided to start over—not by deleting her posts, but by rebuilding her strategy from the ground up. She chose one niche instead of five. She crafted hooks that sparked curiosity. She focused on value instead of aesthetics. She created videos designed to be saved and shared. She learned to batch content and plan around her audience's habits. She stopped trying to impress the algorithm and instead focused on capturing human attention. Within two weeks, her views began to rise. One Reel hit 20,000 views. Another hit 50,000. Followers started arriving daily—slowly at first, then faster. Her content was finally speaking the algorithm's language.

The breakthrough came when one of her Reels entered a new wave of distribution. At first, she thought it was a glitch. Her notifications exploded. Messages poured in. Followers doubled overnight. She didn't realize that Instagram was pushing her video to new audiences because her retention rate was exceptionally high. For the first time, Maya truly understood that growth wasn't about posting more—it was about posting smarter. It was about alignment between the message, the audience, and the algorithm's priorities.

As she grew, she noticed how different her experience felt. She stopped obsessing over perfect visuals and began focusing on creating meaningful content. She realized that people followed her not because of fancy editing, but because she solved problems, shared insights, and spoke clearly to one specific audience. The more she served that audience, the more Instagram rewarded her. Within months, she built a community that trusted her, supported her, and eagerly waited for her next post. Her page became a place of value, not a gallery of random ideas.

Maya's story is not extraordinary; it is proof of what happens when a creator learns how Instagram truly works. She didn't have connections, a professional team, or years of experience. She simply learned the formula and applied it with intention. She realized that Instagram is not a platform reserved for the lucky—it is a platform that rewards creators who understand behavior, consistency, clarity, and value. By mastering these principles, she transformed from invisible to unstoppable.

Her journey mirrors the journey you are beginning right now. Once you understand how Instagram thinks, how the algorithm distributes content, and how audiences decide what to watch, you will never create the same way again. You will have the power to grow intentionally, reach thousands of people, and build a brand that stands the test of time. The chapter you just read is your first step into that transformation, and just like Maya, your rise begins the moment you learn the system behind the success.

Chapter 2

The Psychology of Attention: How to Stop the Scroll and Hook Viewers Instantly

If Chapter 1 explained how Instagram thinks, Chapter 2 explains how humans think—and this is equally important, because the algorithm follows the audience. Every time someone opens Instagram, they enter a rapid-fire decision state, scanning content at high speed and deciding in fractions of a second whether something is worth their attention. Growth on Instagram begins in those tiny moments when someone chooses to pause instead of scroll. This single action—pausing—triggers the entire discovery system. The moment you learn how to influence this decision, your content performance changes forever. Stopping the scroll is not luck; it is a psychological outcome triggered by curiosity, novelty, clarity, or emotional relevance. When you learn how to engineer these triggers, you gain the power to capture attention instantly across Reels, feed posts, and carousel content.

Most creators mistakenly believe that the hook is simply the first sentence or the first frame, but it is far more than that. The hook is not just what people hear or see—it is what they *feel* in the first two seconds. Humans are wired to make quick decisions based on relevance, tension, contrast, or pattern recognition. If the content doesn't signal value immediately, the viewer scrolls away automatically. This is why aesthetic shots, slow intros, or unclear openings fail. The viewer needs instant clarity about what they will get: a problem being solved, a promise being fulfilled, a transformation being revealed, or a piece of information they can't ignore. If the viewer cannot understand the reason to watch right away, retention collapses. Strong hooks always answer the silent question every viewer asks: "Why should I stop for this?"

One of the most powerful ways to stop the scroll is to lead with tension. Tension is created when you disrupt expectations, challenge beliefs, reveal a surprising truth, or expose something people want to know but rarely hear. Openings like "Most people get this completely wrong..." or "Here's the secret nobody talks about..." immediately spark curiosity. Curiosity is the foundation of retention. When the brain senses missing information, it craves closure. This psychological process is known as the "curiosity gap," and it is responsible for some of the most viral Reels on the platform. When you consistently create tension and resolve it clearly, your content becomes addictive.

Another effective attention trigger is **contrast**. The human mind reacts strongly to differences—big vs. small, before vs. after, problem vs. solution, mistake vs. fix. Contrast creates immediate visual interest. This is why quick demonstrations, transformations, and transitions perform extremely well. Viewers instinctively want to understand the shift. Every time you present contrast, you give the brain a reason to stay engaged. For creators in education, finance, fitness, motivation, beauty, or lifestyle niches, contrast becomes a powerful storytelling tool. When used correctly, it not only stops the scroll but increases watch time dramatically.

Clarity is another psychological factor that influences attention. People don't stop for content that feels confusing, vague, or directionless. They stop when they instantly understand what they're about to learn or experience. Clear messaging eliminates hesitation. This is why on-screen text can dramatically improve retention. When the opening text says exactly what the video is about, the viewer can decide immediately whether it's relevant to them. If it is, they stay. If not, they leave—but this helps the algorithm categorize your content faster. Clarity doesn't limit reach; it strengthens it by attracting the right audience and repelling the wrong one.

Creators also underestimate the power of **pattern interruption**, which is the sudden break of a visual or auditory expectation. This could be a quick zoom, a bold phrase on-screen, a surprising statement, a sudden change in angle, or an unexpected sound. Pattern interruption resets the viewer's attention. Because the Instagram feed is repetitive, anything that looks or sounds different creates an attention spike. Humans unconsciously respond to novelty because the brain is constantly searching for meaningful changes in the environment. When your content disrupts predictable patterns, you gain the viewer's focus.

A critical concept in attention psychology is **viewer identity**. People stop scrolling when content speaks directly to who they believe they are—or who they want to become. When your content makes them think, "This is for me," they engage more deeply. Targeted openings such as "If you're trying to grow your page..." or "For anyone struggling with consistency..." instantly activate identity-based attention. The viewer feels seen. This emotional connection increases the likelihood of watching until the end. Every piece of content you create should speak to a specific identity—beginner, entrepreneur, mom, creator, athlete, student, professional, homeowner, traveler, or anyone aligned with your niche.

The most successful hooks combine multiple psychological triggers. A strong opening might use tension, clarity, and identity all at once—for example: "If your Reels keep flopping, here's the real reason they're not working." In this example, the viewer feels tension ("the real reason"), clarity (topic is immediate), and identity (for creators posting Reels). Another powerful combination is curiosity + contrast + value—for example: "I made this one small change and doubled my views overnight." These multi-layered hooks amplify attention and dramatically increase retention.

But stopping the scroll is only the beginning. The next challenge is maintaining attention. Retention is shaped by pacing, relevance, storytelling, editing rhythm, and how quickly the content delivers value. Many creators lose viewers after three to five seconds because the video drags, becomes repetitive, or shifts tones too quickly. Strong retention requires forward movement—every second should lead naturally to the next. This means cutting filler phrases, removing pauses, and tightening sentences. Whenever a viewer senses boredom, they leave. Whenever they sense momentum, they stay. Momentum is the essence of retention.

One important psychological principle is known as **reward frequency**. The viewer should receive small rewards consistently throughout the video—interesting facts, emotional moments, visual changes, humor, insights, or steps. When rewards appear often, the viewer keeps watching. When they appear too late, they leave. The most viral Reels deliver a reward every two to three seconds: new visuals, new angles, new lines, or new insights. Even small shifts keep the dopamine response active. This book will teach you how to engineer reward frequency into every video so your retention becomes unstoppable.

Finally, attention is influenced by **familiarity**. People engage more with creators they recognize. This means your first few videos might struggle until Instagram learns your audience. But once viewers repeatedly see your content and associate you with a specific topic, your retention improves naturally. Familiarity builds trust, and trust increases watch time. This is why consistency accelerates growth—not just because the algorithm likes it, but because the audience responds to repetition and recognizable value.

By understanding the psychology of attention—curiosity, tension, clarity, identity, novelty, pattern interruption, reward frequency, and familiarity—you gain the ability to engineer content that captures viewers immediately and keeps them watching. This chapter is your blueprint for designing powerful openings, strategic storytelling, and highly engaging Reels that outperform the competition. Attention is the currency of Instagram. When you master it, everything else becomes easier: reach, followers, sales, brand deals, and community. Growth begins with a pause—and you now control the pause.

"Two Seconds That Changed Everything"

Elias had been posting on Instagram for months without making any real progress. His videos were polished, his captions thoughtful, and his hashtags researched, yet his Reels rarely gained more than a few hundred views. He didn't understand how other creators with less experience and less quality seemed to explode overnight while he felt invisible. What he didn't realize was that his content looked great but didn't *hook* anyone. It didn't stop the scroll. The first two seconds were too slow, too soft, too predictable. They didn't spark curiosity or emotion. They didn't give viewers a reason to stay. Elias poured effort into everything except the most important part—the beginning.

One night, while scrolling, he noticed something unusual. He watched a Reel from a creator with low-quality lighting and casual editing, yet it had hundreds of thousands of views. The opening line grabbed him instantly: "If you're struggling to stay motivated, listen to this." That one sentence pulled him in. He watched to the end. Then he watched another. Suddenly, he realized that he kept stopping for videos that spoke directly to him, challenged his assumptions, or created tension immediately. These openings didn't just attract his eyes—they awakened something inside him. For the first time, he began to understand why his content wasn't working.

The next day, Elias decided to study the first two seconds of every viral Reel he came across. He noticed patterns he had never seen before. Some creators used shocking facts. Others started with bold statements. Some used text on-screen with a clear promise. Others used unexpected visuals that snapped the viewer's attention. Every successful video had one thing in common—it forced the viewer to pause. That simple pause was the doorway to everything: retention, engagement, discovery, and new followers. He had been focusing on transitions and editing when he should have been focusing on psychology.

Feeling inspired, Elias rewrote his next Reel from scratch. He removed the slow intro, tightened the script, added on-screen text, and led with a statement that he knew his audience needed to hear: "You're not failing—you're trying without a strategy." He filmed it quickly, uploaded it, and walked away without expecting much. Hours later, he returned to his phone to find hundreds of notifications. His video had broken his record for views. People were saving it, sharing it, commenting, and following him. What changed wasn't his editing skills—it was his understanding of human behavior.

As days passed, Elias began experimenting with different attention triggers. He tried curiosity gaps like "Most people get this wrong..." and noticed viewers stayed longer. He tried contrast clips showing "before and after" transformations and saw engagement spike. He used identity-based openings like "If you're trying to build your confidence..." and watched followers pour in. Every time he aligned his hook with psychology, the results improved. He didn't need fancy equipment. He didn't need a team. He didn't need perfect visuals. What he needed was clarity, momentum, and emotional relevance.

His biggest breakthrough happened when he posted a Reel that started with, "This is why your goals keep failing." The video wasn't complex. It had no special effects. But it had tension and clarity. It spoke directly to a pain point. It delivered value quickly. That Reel went viral, reaching hundreds of thousands of viewers. For the first time in his life, Elias felt what it was like to have his content resonate with strangers around the world. His follower count surged. Brands reached out. People thanked him for his words. His page, once invisible, had become magnetic.

Through this journey, Elias learned that success on Instagram wasn't about being the best editor or the most photogenic creator. It was about understanding how humans think and what makes them care. He realized that attention is a gift—and you must earn it. When he mastered the psychology behind those first two seconds, everything else transformed. He no longer feared the algorithm. He no longer felt lost. He knew exactly what to do, because he understood the moment where all growth begins: the moment someone decides to stop scrolling.

As he continued posting, Elias became living proof that anyone can grow when they learn to capture attention. His confidence grew with every video, not because of views, but because he finally understood the system. He began to see opportunities everywhere—inside conversations, experiences, struggles, and lessons. Everything became content. Everything became a hook. Everything became a chance to help someone. Those two seconds didn't just change his videos—they changed his entire trajectory.

His story shows what is possible when a creator learns the psychology of attention. You can have the same transformation. The moment you learn how to stop the scroll, you take control of your growth. The moment you master curiosity, clarity, tension, and identity, you unlock the true power of Instagram. The next viral video, the next audience breakthrough, the next surge of followers—it all begins in the first two seconds. And now, you know how to create them.

Chapter 3

Crafting Your Niche: Positioning Yourself for Maximum Growth & Algorithm Clarity

One of the biggest reasons creators struggle on Instagram is that they haven't defined their niche clearly enough for the algorithm—or for the audience—to understand what they represent. In the world of short attention spans, people need instant clarity about who you are and what your content offers. When your topic feels scattered, inconsistent, or unfocused, both the algorithm and the audience become confused. Confusion is the enemy of growth. Clarity is the catalyst. Your niche is not just your topic—it's your message, your identity, your value, and your positioning. It is the foundation that tells Instagram exactly who to recommend your content to, and it tells viewers why they should follow you instead of the thousands of other creators posting daily. Without a niche, growth feels random. With a niche, growth becomes predictable.

A niche is not meant to restrict you; it is meant to amplify you. Many creators fear choosing a niche because they believe it will limit what they can talk about, but the opposite is true. A niche multiplies your reach because it gives people a reason to stay. When they know what to expect from you, they engage more, return more, and follow more confidently. Instagram's recommendation system works the same way. It categorizes your page based on the topics you post most consistently. When you stay within a core niche, Instagram quickly learns that your content is relevant to a specific type of viewer, which makes it easier for the algorithm to deliver your videos to the right audience—people who are most likely to engage, save, share, and follow. This creates a feedback loop that accelerates discovery.

Choosing the right niche requires understanding the intersection of three elements: what you can teach, what you enjoy, and what people already want. This intersection is where sustainable growth happens. If you choose a niche only because it's trending, you risk burnout. If you choose a niche only because you enjoy it, you risk low demand. If you choose a niche purely based on what people want, you risk lacking authenticity or expertise. But when your niche blends purpose, passion, and demand, your content becomes easier to create and easier to consume. This chapter will help you identify that sweet spot so you can grow efficiently and authentically.

Your niche should be structured like a pyramid. At the top is your main niche category—for example: fitness, beauty, real estate, finance, cooking, motivation, wellness, lifestyle, travel, parenting, entrepreneurship, or personal development. Below the top layer is your sub-niche, which narrows your focus. For example, “fitness” becomes “home workouts for busy professionals.” “Beauty” becomes “easy makeup tutorials for beginners.” “Finance” becomes “credit tips for young adults.” “Cooking” becomes “quick meals for families.” Sub-niches help you stand out immediately. They tell viewers and the algorithm exactly who the content is for.

The third layer of your niche is your content angle—your unique perspective or approach. Two creators can share the same niche but grow differently because of their angle. One fitness creator may focus on injury-friendly exercises, another on bodyweight workouts, another on science-based training, and another on motivation. One finance creator may focus on budgeting, another on credit building, another on investing, and another on side hustles. Your angle is what makes your page recognizable even if your topic is not unique. People don’t follow general content; they follow perspectives. When your angle is clear, you become memorable.

The fourth layer is your content style. This includes your tone, your editing rhythm, your messaging, your on-screen presence, your pacing, and your storytelling structure. Some creators are rapid-fire and energetic. Others are calm and thoughtful. Some use text-heavy formats. Others rely on visuals. Some creators speak on camera, while others stay faceless. The algorithm does not require you to show your face to grow. It only requires consistency in your style so it can categorize your content type. A consistent style trains the viewer to know what to expect, and predictability increases retention.

Once you've identified your niche structure, the next step is choosing your content pillars—three to five repeatable content themes you rotate through regularly. Content pillars give your page structure and prevent you from running out of ideas. If your brand is fitness, your pillars might be workouts, nutrition, motivation, and mobility. If your niche is real estate, your pillars might be home tours, buying tips, mortgage insights, and market trends. If your niche is motivation, your pillars might be mindset, habits, discipline, and goal-setting. When your content follows clear pillars, viewers understand your value instantly.

Your niche also influences your hooks, captions, hashtags, and retention strategies. When you know exactly who you speak to, your messaging becomes sharper. Instead of vague hooks like "Here's a tip," you produce powerful identity-based hooks like "If you're trying to build your credit..." or "If you struggle to stay consistent at the gym..." The more specific your audience feels, the deeper the connection. Broad content feels like noise.

Targeted content feels like guidance. Creators often assume their niche is too small or too competitive, but every niche has endless depth because people join platforms every day. The key is not to find the smallest niche but the clearest one. A clear niche does not limit future expansion. In fact, once you grow, you can expand naturally into broader topics because your audience trusts you. But at the start, narrow beats wide. Focus beats generality. Clarity beats creativity. Choose your niche intentionally now so you can grow exponentially later.

As you refine your niche, remember this: people follow accounts that help them solve problems, achieve goals, avoid mistakes, feel inspired, or improve their identity. Your niche should connect directly to one of these outcomes. If your page improves someone's life—even slightly—they will follow you. When your niche becomes a source of transformation, your content begins to spread far beyond your existing audience. Transformation is the most powerful niche of all.

By the end of this chapter, you should have complete clarity about who you serve, what you offer, and why your audience should follow you. Your niche is the backbone of your brand, the structure that organizes your content, and the signal that teaches Instagram exactly where to send your videos. Once your niche becomes clear, the rest of your Instagram strategy becomes easier—your hooks, your scripts, your visuals, your captions, and your posting rhythm all fall into place. Growth no longer feels random. It becomes intentional. And with intention comes momentum.

"The Niche That Changed Everything"

For months, Aria felt lost on Instagram. She posted beauty tips one day, travel clips the next, fitness videos the following week, and motivational quotes whenever she felt inspired. Her profile looked like a scrapbook of ideas rather than a cohesive brand. Her views were inconsistent, her follower count barely moved, and every time she tried something new, it felt like starting from zero again. She admired creators who seemed to grow effortlessly, but deep down she believed they had something she didn't—confidence, charisma, better looks, better editing, or simply more luck. She didn't realize the real reason she struggled was far simpler: she had not chosen a niche.

One afternoon, while scrolling through Instagram, she noticed a creator named Lena whose page was growing rapidly. Lena didn't have fancy equipment or perfect lighting. She didn't post a wide mix of topics. Instead, she focused on one thing: simple skincare routines for people with sensitive skin. Every video had the same style, the same tone, and the same message. Aria watched a few Reels and suddenly understood why Lena was exploding—viewers instantly knew what her page was about. There was no confusion. No guessing. No randomness. Lena had carved out a niche so clear that the algorithm and the audience knew exactly where to place her.

Curious, Aria decided to review her own page. For the first time, she saw it through the viewer's eyes. She realized that if she didn't know herself well enough to define her content, how could viewers possibly know what she stood for? She remembered her own experience on Instagram—she only followed creators who offered specific value. She followed fitness creators for tips, cooking creators for recipes, finance creators for guidance, and beauty creators for tutorials. People follow clarity. She had been offering chaos.

Determined to change, Aria sat down with a notebook and made three lists: what she enjoyed teaching, what she was naturally good at, and what people constantly asked her about. One topic stood out on all three lists—simple, sustainable wellness routines. She realized she didn't have to choose between fitness, beauty, and motivation. She could combine them under one niche: wellness for busy women. It felt effortless, aligned, and true. For the first time, she felt excited instead of overwhelmed.

Aria restructured her entire page. She updated her bio, redefined her content pillars, and planned her next ten Reels based on her new direction. Her hooks became sharper. Her messaging became clearer. Her scripts felt easier to write because they all served the same purpose. She posted her first Reel in her new niche with a hook that said, “If you’re a busy woman trying to take care of yourself, this is for you.” It wasn’t her most aesthetic video, but it was her most focused. And that focus made all the difference.

The Reel performed better than anything she had posted in months. Viewers commented things like “This is exactly what I needed” and “Finally someone speaking to me!” For the first time, she felt a connection with her audience. They weren’t just watching; they were resonating. They felt seen. They felt understood. And they followed her—not because she was perfect, but because she was specific.

Over the next few weeks, her page transformed. Her views increased steadily. Her comments became meaningful. Her followers grew. She didn’t feel like she was starting over with every post anymore. She felt like she was building something—something with structure, purpose, and identity. Every piece of content reinforced her message. Every Reel strengthened her relationship with her niche. And every day, Instagram’s algorithm learned exactly who her ideal audience was.

Her breakthrough came when one of her morning routine Reels went viral. It reached hundreds of thousands of viewers, gained thousands of shares, and brought in a wave of followers. People messaged her saying her content made their lives easier. Aria couldn't believe how quickly everything changed, all because she defined her niche. She used to believe other creators had advantages she didn't—but she realized the only real advantage was clarity. When she found clarity, she found momentum. And once momentum arrived, everything became easier.

Aria's rise wasn't luck. It wasn't timing. It wasn't perfect editing. It was niche alignment. Her story proves a simple truth: you don't need to be unique to succeed. You need to be clear. When you choose your niche with intention, the algorithm understands you. The audience appreciates you. And your content finally finds its home. That clarity changed everything for Aria—and it will change everything for you, too.

Chapter 4

Mastering Reels: The Content Format That Drives the Fastest Growth

Reels are the single most powerful growth vehicle on Instagram, and understanding how to use them strategically is one of the most important skills you can develop as a creator. No other content format gives you equal access to new audiences regardless of your follower count. Reels place beginners and experienced creators on the same playing field, allowing anyone to reach thousands or even millions of people if their content meets the right engagement thresholds. If your goal is to grow fast, expand your reach, and gain new followers consistently, mastering Reels is not optional—it is essential. But successful Reels do not happen by accident. They follow a predictable structure built around attention, retention, value, and clarity. Once you understand that structure, your growth becomes dramatically easier.

Reels succeed for one core reason: they align perfectly with how the human brain consumes information. People scroll quickly, make decisions instantly, and have limited patience. Short-form video satisfies the need for rapid stimulation, clear messaging, and fast delivery of value. The algorithm knows this and prioritizes Reels heavily because they keep viewers inside the app longer. Every time you create a Reel that holds attention, Instagram rewards you with more visibility. This means that Reels are not random; they are simply the platform's most efficient way of identifying which creators can engage audiences at scale. Your job is to understand what makes viewers stay and what makes them leave.

A high-performing Reel has four core components: the hook, the body, the pacing, and the payoff. The hook determines whether the viewer stays. The body determines whether they keep watching. The pacing determines whether they remain engaged. And the payoff determines whether they like, save, share, or follow. If any one of these components is weak, retention drops and distribution slows. If they are all strong, distribution expands in waves. Most creators fail because they focus on editing instead of structure. Editing can enhance a video, but structure is what determines its success. A messy edit with a perfect structure will outperform a polished edit with weak messaging every time.

The hook is the most important element of any Reel. It should immediately tell the viewer what to expect or spark curiosity so strong that they must continue watching. Hooks can be delivered through on-screen text, spoken words, or a visually surprising moment, but they must be clear. Ambiguous openings kill retention. Examples of strong hooks include "If you're struggling with this, watch," "Here's what no one tells you...," "This is the mistake that stops people from reaching their goals," or "Try this instead of wasting hours doing it the hard way." Whether your niche is fitness, wellness, real estate, finance, beauty, lifestyle, or motivation, you can craft hooks that speak directly to the identities and desires of your target audience. The more specific your hook, the stronger the retention.

After the hook, the body of the Reel must maintain tension and momentum. The biggest reason viewers drop off is stagnation. If the content does not evolve every couple of seconds, the viewer loses interest. This means your scripting must be tight, your sentences must be concise, and your visuals must support your message. Avoid long pauses, unnecessary intros, repetitive statements, and slow movements. Every second should add something new—new information, new emotions, new visuals, new steps, or new angles. This constant refresh is what drives retention upward and tells the algorithm that your content deserves larger distribution.

Pacing is another critical element. Good pacing does not mean rushing. It means eliminating filler. It means speaking with clarity and certainty. It means editing your videos so the flow is seamless and natural. Fast-paced Reels work well when delivering tips, tutorials, or transformations. Medium-paced

Reels work well for emotional storytelling or lifestyle content. Slow-paced Reels work only when the visuals are compelling enough to hold attention without verbal guidance. The key is matching your pacing to the content type so the viewer stays engaged from start to finish.

The payoff is the final part of the Reel, and it determines how the viewer reacts. Payoffs create emotional resolution. They can inspire, surprise, teach, or encourage action. Examples include revealing the final step of a transformation, giving a practical takeaway, showing a before-and-after result, sharing a quick recap, or providing a call-to-action such as "Save this for later," "Share this with someone who needs it," or "Follow for more tips like this." A strong payoff increases engagement depth, which boosts the algorithm's confidence in your content. Payoffs are also essential for converting viewers into followers.

Another important factor in Reel performance is watch time. Instagram favors videos that are watched more than once or watched all the way to the end. This means shorter Reels often perform better than longer ones, especially for creators still building their momentum. A 7-second Reel with perfect retention can outperform a 20-second Reel with weaker retention. It's not about length—it's about efficiency. Once your content consistently holds attention, you can begin experimenting with longer durations. Using text on-screen is one of the easiest ways to enhance clarity and retention. On-screen text helps people understand the topic quickly, anchors attention, and makes the Reel accessible to viewers who watch without sound. It also helps Instagram categorize your content through visual keyword recognition. The strongest Reels use text that matches the hook and summarizes the benefit of watching. Your text should be simple, bold, and easy to read. Avoid cluttered fonts or excessive wording. A few well-chosen words can transform your engagement.

Finally, consistency is vital for mastering Reels. You don't need to post every day, but you should maintain a rhythm that teaches the algorithm who you are. Three to four Reels per week is often enough to build steady growth. When you show up consistently, Instagram learns your patterns, understands your niche, and begins recommending your content more aggressively. Your audience also becomes more familiar with your voice, style, and message, which drives deeper engagement.

Reels are not just a trend—they are the backbone of modern Instagram growth. They give you leverage, speed, and access to audience segments that would otherwise take years to reach. The more you simplify your process, refine your structure, and understand your audience's psychology, the faster your Reels will grow. Once you master hooks, pacing, structure, and payoff, your content becomes magnetic—and growth becomes the natural result.

"The Reel That Changed His Life"

For months, Daniel watched other creators gain traction while his own content received minimal views. He spent hours filming, editing, color-grading, and adding transitions, yet the results never matched his effort. His videos looked polished, but they didn't spread. They didn't capture attention. They didn't convert viewers into followers. He assumed Instagram was oversaturated or that the algorithm was working against him. But the truth was simpler—his Reels were beautiful but ineffective. They lacked the structure that made people stop, stay, and engage.

One evening, frustrated and exhausted, Daniel stumbled across a Reel from a young creator who had gained tens of thousands of followers seemingly overnight. The video was simple: no fancy editing, no transitions, no professional lighting. But the opening line was powerful—"Here's the mistake everyone makes when trying to improve their life." Daniel paused without thinking. The video held him. It spoke directly to him. It delivered value quickly. When it ended, he watched it again. And again. Suddenly, he understood: it wasn't the polish that mattered. It was the psychology behind the structure.

Inspired, Daniel decided to experiment. He studied high-performing Reels obsessively, not for their visuals but for their messaging. He realized every viral Reel had the same components: a compelling hook, a clear body, engaging pacing, and a satisfying payoff. He recognized how each element influenced behavior. He analyzed the hooks that stopped him. He examined the sentences that kept him watching. He noticed how creators used text to anchor attention and how they resolved their message with clarity. He saw patterns he had never noticed before.

The next morning, he rewrote his content strategy. He scrapped his old scripts and replaced them with crisp, powerful hooks. He removed filler sentences. He simplified his visuals. He added bold, clear on-screen text to signal the topic instantly. Most importantly, he focused on delivering value within the first second. His next Reel began with the line, "If you feel stuck, here's the truth nobody tells you." He filmed it in one take, edited it lightly, and posted it with low expectations.

A few hours later, his notifications blew up.

The Reel had broken every record he had. It reached tens of

thousands of viewers, then hundreds of thousands. Comments poured in. People shared it. People saved it. People followed him. For the first time in his life, Daniel felt what it was like to speak directly to an audience that cared. He realized he had been focusing on the wrong things for months. It wasn't about perfection—it was about connection.

Over the next few weeks, Daniel refined his approach. He crafted hooks that addressed real problems. He used concise scripting. He increased pacing. He added meaningful payoffs. Every time he improved one component of his structure, retention increased. His Reels became more powerful, more transformative, and more relatable. As a result, his page grew faster than he had ever imagined.

The real breakthrough came when a Reel he almost didn't post went viral worldwide. In it, he spoke honestly, without overthinking. The hook was simple, the pacing smooth, the message impactful. That one Reel reached millions. Opportunities appeared overnight. Brands reached out. Collaborations started. Followers commented daily about how his content had helped them. Daniel realized that mastering Reels wasn't just about growth—it was about impact.

His transformation wasn't luck. It wasn't timing. It was understanding how Reels work at the deepest level. Daniel learned that Reels amplify clarity, value, and authenticity. When creators stop trying to impress and start trying to help, everything changes. His journey reflects what happens when a creator learns the structure behind the success. Once he mastered Reels, he unlocked a new world of possibilities—visibility, opportunity, income, and influence.

That one Reel didn't just change his platform. It changed his life.

Chapter 5

Content Timing & Frequency: When to Post for Maximum Reach and Rapid Growth

One of the most misunderstood aspects of Instagram growth is timing. Many creators spend countless hours perfecting their edits, refining their hooks, and polishing their visuals, only to post at a time when their audience isn't active and the algorithm has fewer engagement signals to work with. Timing is not the most important factor in growth, but it is a powerful amplifier. A great post at the wrong time gets less initial traction, and the algorithm uses that early performance to determine whether the content deserves wider distribution. Posting at the right time boosts your early reach, accelerates engagement, and gives your content a stronger chance of entering larger distribution waves. Timing is not about luck. It is about understanding viewer behavior, daily patterns, and algorithmic rhythms that influence how long your content stays in circulation.

Instagram prioritizes fresh content—especially Reels—when determining what to show users. This means the first hour after posting is critical. If your core audience is active during that window, you benefit from higher engagement density, which sends a positive signal to the algorithm. If your audience is inactive, your content enters the system quietly, receiving lower engagement volume and weaker testing results. Many creators misinterpret weak initial engagement as a content problem, when in reality it may be a timing issue. The algorithm evaluates early momentum, and timing directly influences that momentum.

Understanding your audience's activity is the foundation of optimal timing. Your followers have patterns—periods when they check their phones, scroll longer, engage more deeply, or prefer certain types of content. Most people are active in the morning, during lunch breaks, mid-afternoon, early evening, and late at night. But the exact timing depends on your niche, your target demographic, and your audience's lifestyle. Business professionals often scroll early morning and after work. Students and young adults tend to scroll late at night. Parents scroll mid-morning or during quiet evening hours. Entrepreneurs scroll throughout the day. When you align your posting schedule with your audience's rhythm, you increase your chances of capturing attention and boosting initial engagement.

Instagram Insights provides valuable data about follower activity. Instead of choosing random posting times or relying on generalized advice, study your own analytics. Look for the hours when your audience is most active. Posting one hour before peak activity allows your content to warm up before the majority of your audience arrives. This ensures your content is already circulating, gaining momentum, and positioned for discovery when your followers log in. This approach consistently improves early engagement and makes your posts more discoverable.

Frequency plays a major role in growth as well. Many creators feel pressured to post every single day because they believe quantity equals success. While posting frequently can help the algorithm understand your niche and content style, posting too often can lead to creative burnout and lower-quality content. Consistency matters more than frequency. A balanced rhythm of three to five Reels per week is enough to build strong growth without overwhelming yourself. If you force yourself to post daily at the expense of quality, your retention drops, your engagement weakens, and your reach suffers. It is better to post fewer high-performing Reels than to overload your feed with content that doesn't resonate.

Another key aspect of timing is content type. People consume different kinds of content at different times of day. Educational videos perform well earlier in the day when viewers feel focused. Motivational content performs strongly in the morning or evening when people reflect on goals.

Lifestyle content performs well midday. Entertainment content often peaks late evening when viewers relax. Understanding these rhythms helps you pair your content with your viewers' mental state, increasing relevance and engagement.

The concept of "posting windows" is another valuable tool for growth. Posting windows are recurring time blocks when your content tends to perform best. These windows may differ depending on your niche, your geographic audience, and your consistency. Once you identify two or three high-performing windows, rotate your content through those slots instead of guessing. Posting during familiar windows trains both the audience and the algorithm to expect your content at predictable times, which strengthens engagement patterns over time.

Momentum is another factor connected to timing. The algorithm rewards creators who produce consistent engagement over weeks, not just isolated peaks. This means your posting schedule should be sustainable. If you post heavily for one week and vanish for two, your growth becomes unstable. But if you post steadily over a long period, the algorithm becomes more confident in your content and delivers it more aggressively. Viewers also develop familiarity when they see your content regularly. Familiarity increases both retention and engagement. The timing of your interactions also influences reach. Engaging with your followers—replying to comments, responding to DMs, or posting Stories—before and after posting can increase your visibility. These activities signal to Instagram that your account is active and that your audience is engaged with you, which can strengthen your post's initial performance. Additionally, creating a short Story that previews or supports your Reel can remind your followers to engage with your new content.

Creators often overlook the importance of time zones. If your audience is spread across multiple regions, your posting windows need to reflect the largest or most engaged segment. For example, if your niche reaches both U.S. and European audiences, posting at times when both regions are active can increase global reach. If your audience is primarily local, timing becomes simpler. The goal is to align with the behavior of your most active followers.

Ultimately, timing is a multiplier—not a creator of success. Great content posted at the wrong time may struggle, but great content posted at the right time can explode. The combination of strong structure, value-driven messaging, and optimal timing creates the ideal environment for rapid growth. When you master timing and frequency, you give your content a powerful boost, helping it pass early engagement tests, enter new distribution waves, and reach audiences that otherwise might never have found you.

"The Hour That Made All the Difference"

Camila had been posting on Instagram consistently, but her engagement was unpredictable. Some days her Reels performed well; other days they barely reached a fraction of her followers. She couldn't understand why. She spent countless hours refining her content, improving her hooks, and polishing her editing skills, yet the results still fluctuated. She assumed the algorithm was unstable or that her niche was too saturated. But the truth revealed itself unexpectedly one evening.

One night, Camila opened her analytics out of frustration and noticed something she had never paid attention to before—her follower activity graph. The peak hours were clear: her audience was most active in the evening. But she had always posted early morning, assuming it was "optimal." She didn't realize she had been competing with content posted by larger creators who dominated those early time slots. Worse, she had been posting when her specific audience wasn't even online. She had been setting her content up for weak initial engagement without knowing it.

Determined to test a new approach, Camila posted her next Reel one hour before her peak evening window. She didn't expect much, but she wanted to try. Within minutes, her notifications lit up faster than usual. Comments appeared quickly. Likes came in steadily. The Reel entered its first distribution wave stronger than anything she had ever posted before. She watched in awe as her view count climbed—steady, consistent, and far higher than she was used to. That evening, she realized the power of timing.

Over the next week, Camila tested different posting windows. She posted during lunchtime, mid-afternoon, and late evening. She tracked every performance, noted patterns, and discovered that her audience engaged best in two specific windows. She didn't need to guess anymore. She had data. She had clarity. For the first time in her creator journey, her posting schedule felt intentional instead of random. Every time she posted during these windows, her content gained faster traction, stronger engagement, and smoother distribution.

One evening, while preparing her next post, she noticed something interesting. She had replied to comments and posted a Story earlier that day, and her audience had been unusually interactive. She wondered if her pre-post engagement would impact her Reel's performance. She decided to post soon after. The results surprised her. The Reel's early engagement was significantly stronger than usual. It became clear that the algorithm responded positively when her account showed signs of recent activity. Her followers also seemed more eager to engage when they had interacted with her earlier. Camila's breakthrough came when she combined everything she had learned—her optimized posting window, her active engagement routine, and her consistent schedule. She posted a simple morning routine Reel during her highest engagement window. It wasn't her flashiest edit or her boldest message, but it reached thousands more viewers than her typical content. The Reel entered a second wave, then a third. Over the next 72 hours, the video went viral within her niche. Her follower count surged. People messaged her daily, thanking her for the value she provided. For the first time, Camila felt the momentum she had always dreamed of.

As her page grew, she realized timing wasn't just about posting content—it was about posting content when viewers were mentally ready to receive it. She learned that educational content thrived earlier in the day when people felt focused, while motivational content performed better in the evening when people reflected on their day. She paired content types with the right mental states, and her engagement skyrocketed. She wasn't lucky. She was strategic.

Weeks rolled into months, and Camila's page continued to grow steadily. She no longer feared inconsistent engagement because she understood the rhythms of her audience. She had transformed timing from a mystery into a method. She had discovered the hour that made all the difference—and it changed everything.

Her story is a reminder that growth is not just about creating great content. It's about delivering that content when your audience is ready to see it. Timing doesn't just amplify reach—it amplifies opportunity. And once you master it, you create a predictable pattern of visibility that compounds into long-term growth.

Chapter 6

Creating High-Value Content: What Makes People Save, Share, Follow, and Come Back

The true engine of Instagram growth is not simply posting consistently–it is posting content that people consider "high value." High-value content is the kind of content viewers remember, revisit, save for later, share with others, and follow you because of. It goes beyond aesthetics or entertainment. It creates impact. It solves problems. It changes perspectives. It teaches something. It triggers emotion. It offers clarity. High-value content makes a viewer feel like their life became easier, better, smarter, more inspired, or more capable because of your post. When content adds value, it spreads naturally. When content lacks value, even perfect editing or timing cannot save it. Value is the foundation of long-term growth.

High-value content can take five primary forms: educational, inspirational, emotional, transformational, or relatable. Educational content teaches the viewer something practical or useful. Inspirational content motivates them to improve or begin something. Emotional content resonates with feelings, struggles, or personal experiences. Transformational content shows a before-and-after or a major insight. Relatable content makes the viewer think, “This is exactly how I feel,” which builds connection. While entertainment also performs well, these five value categories consistently create deeper engagement—especially saves and shares, the strongest algorithmic signals.

The core of high-value content is relevance. Your content must address a problem, desire, question, frustration, or aspiration your audience already has. When your niche is clear, your value becomes easy to define. For example, in fitness, high-value content includes workouts, meal ideas, form corrections, or motivation. In finance, high-value content includes budgeting tips, credit strategies, or money mistakes to avoid. In beauty, value includes tutorials, product comparisons, or simple routines. In motivation, value includes mindset shifts, habits, daily challenges, or self-reflection insights. When your content directly serves your niche’s needs, engagement increases naturally.

Saves are the strongest form of engagement because they signal long-term value. People save content they want to revisit. This includes tutorials, checklists, reminders, tips, and step-by-step guides. If you want more saves, focus on clarity and practicality. Make your information simple to follow. Use text on-screen to break down steps. Avoid overwhelming the viewer with complexity. The easier your content is to apply, the more likely people will save it.

Shares drive discovery. When people share your Reel with a friend, they are telling the algorithm your content is meaningful and relevant. People share content that feels insightful, surprising, emotional, funny, or relatable. They also share content that delivers tiny “aha moments”—the kind of moments that make them think, “I wish someone told me this earlier.” If you want more shares, focus on perspective shifts, valuable truths, or universal experiences.

Follows occur when a viewer believes your page can improve their life consistently. This means your content must make a strong promise: “You will benefit if you keep watching me.” Follows are not earned by one good video—they are earned by consistent themes, clear messaging, and repeated value. To increase follows, you must speak to identity—the kind of person your audience wants to be. Hooks like “If you're trying to fix X...” or “If you want to improve Y...” attract people who desire transformation. When your content aligns with their identity, following becomes automatic.

High-value content is built on clarity. If your message is unclear, viewers leave. Clarity means delivering one specific idea—not multiple ideas—in one Reel. Many creators try to cram too much into one video, diluting the message. A clear video has one message, one transformation, and one takeaway. This makes it more impactful, easier to follow, and more likely to be saved or shared. When viewers know exactly what they're getting, retention increases.

Specificity is another essential ingredient. Generic advice feels empty. Specific advice feels powerful. "Drink water" is generic. "Drink one glass of water before every meal to reset cravings and prevent overeating" is specific. "Build your credit" is vague. "Increase your credit score by paying off small balances first and lowering your credit utilization below 30%" is specific. Specific content feels actionable and trustworthy. This makes your audience more likely to engage deeply and follow you.

High-value content also needs emotional connection. People are more likely to save or share when they feel something—hope, motivation, relief, clarity, confidence, inspiration, or even discomfort. Emotion multiplies value. You can trigger emotion through personal stories, relatable struggles, vulnerable insights, honest truths, or bold statements. The strongest content blends value with emotion—teaching something while making viewers feel understood.

One of the most effective frameworks for high-value content is the "Problem → Insight → Solution" structure. Begin by identifying a problem your audience faces. Offer insight that reframes the problem or reveals something unexpected. End with a solution or practical step. This structure is powerful because it creates relevance, surprise, and utility—all in one video. It keeps retention high and increases engagement.

Another framework is "Mistake → Explanation → Better Way." People are curious about what they are doing wrong. Mistake-based content grabs attention immediately because it creates tension. When you reveal a better way, you deliver value and resolution. This format consistently drives saves and shares.

Transformational content is also powerful. Showing a before-and-after—whether physical, emotional, financial, or skill-based—illustrates value visually. Transformation is one of the strongest psychological triggers. It shows possibility. It inspires belief. It makes viewers want the same result. Transformation videos tend to gain followers faster than informational videos because they connect with the viewer's desire for improvement.

Finally, authenticity enhances value. People connect with real stories, real insights, real struggles, and real lessons. Authentic content builds trust, and trust builds long-term engagement. You don't need to reveal everything about your life, but showing genuine emotion, honesty, and humanity makes your content more relatable. Your audience is not just looking for information; they're looking for connection.

High-value content is the foundation for sustainable growth. When your content consistently improves someone's life, even in small ways, people return to your page. They save your videos. They share your insights. They follow your journey. They trust your voice. When you master value, you don't just gain reach—you gain influence. And with influence comes opportunity, monetization, and long-term success.

"The Video That Made People Care"

Nina had been creating content for months, but her videos never truly resonated. People watched for a few seconds and scrolled away. Some liked her Reels, but few saved or shared them. Her follower count barely moved. She knew she was working hard, but she wasn't working effectively. Deep down, she felt invisible. Her content looked good, but it lacked something she couldn't name. She didn't realize the missing piece was value.

One day, Nina posted a Reel about her morning routine. It was beautifully edited with aesthetic shots, calming music, and nice transitions. But when she checked her analytics later, the retention was terrible. People clicked away almost immediately. She felt discouraged. She wondered why aesthetic creators went viral while she struggled. But as she scrolled through Instagram that night, she noticed something interesting. Her favorite creators weren't just aesthetic—they were impactful. They taught her something new. They inspired her. They helped her. They made her feel something. Their content wasn't about looking good—it was about providing value.

The next morning, Nina had a realization. She had been posting for herself—not for the viewer. Her content didn't solve a problem, answer a question, or offer insight. It was pretty but empty. She understood why people didn't save it, share it, or follow her because of it. She wasn't giving them a reason to care.

Determined to change, she studied high-value creators. She analyzed what made their content powerful. She noticed how they broke down steps clearly. How they addressed common struggles. How they framed insights in simple, memorable ways. How they used text to guide the viewer. How they shared personal stories that felt real. How they made the viewer feel understood. Nina realized that value wasn't complicated—it was intentional.

She decided to test a new approach. She created a Reel about something she personally struggled with: staying consistent. Instead of filming aesthetic shots, she spoke directly to the viewer with a clear message: "If you struggle to stay consistent, here's the mindset shift that changed everything." She shared an insight she wished someone had told her earlier. She added on-screen text for clarity. She kept the video simple, but meaningful. She didn't expect much—but she felt different posting it.

Within hours, comments flooded in. People thanked her. People said they needed to hear it. People saved it. People shared it with friends. For the first time, Nina felt like she had made an impact. It wasn't the visuals—it was the value. She had created something that genuinely helped people.

Encouraged, she began creating more high-value content. She shared tips that had helped her. She talked about mistakes she made on her journey. She offered solutions, insights, and small steps her audience could apply instantly. Every video had a purpose. Every message had intention. Her content became clearer, stronger, and more focused. She stopped trying to impress and started trying to serve.

The more value she provided, the more her audience grew. People trusted her. They returned to her page regularly. They commented more deeply. They engaged more meaningfully. Her saves and shares skyrocketed. Her follower count began climbing consistently. Opportunities appeared—brand partnerships, collaborations, and conversations she never imagined possible.

Her breakthrough came when she created a Reel that simply said, “If you’ve been struggling lately, this is for you.” She shared a raw truth that she herself had needed to hear. The video exploded. It went viral. It reached millions. People around the world resonated with her words. They shared it endlessly. That single Reel changed everything for her.

Nina realized that high-value content isn’t about perfection—it’s about connection. It’s about making someone’s life a little better in the few seconds they spend with your video. Her story shows that the moment you focus on value, people begin to care. They engage. They follow. They support you. And you become the creator they trust.

Chapter 7

The Explore Page Formula: How to Get Instagram to Recommend Your Content to Thousands

The Explore page is one of the most powerful discovery engines on Instagram, yet most creators misunderstand how it works or assume it's reserved for accounts with massive followings. In reality, the Explore page rewards creators who consistently demonstrate strong engagement patterns, clear niche identity, high value, and predictable audience behavior. The Explore page is not about luck–it is about alignment. When your content aligns with what viewers in your niche want, Instagram identifies your posts as "high recommendation candidates," meaning the algorithm sees your content as likely to perform well with similar audiences. Once you unlock this, growth accelerates because the Explore page places your content in front of thousands of non-followers who are already primed to engage.

The Explore page uses a recommendation system that evaluates three main factors: the relevance of your content, the performance of your content, and the behavior of your audience. Relevance means your content matches what users with similar interests are actively engaging with. Performance means your content performs better than average during its initial testing phase. Audience behavior means the people who already follow you engage consistently with your posts. When you understand these three elements, you begin to engineer your content for recommendation rather than hoping for it.

Relevance begins with niche clarity. If your niche is inconsistent, the algorithm struggles to categorize your content. When your posts fit cleanly within one niche and follow consistent themes, Instagram learns quickly who your ideal viewer is. For example, if you post finance tips, credit building strategies, and budgeting content consistently, Instagram knows your content is relevant to users who engage with financial education. If you post fitness content regularly, Instagram recommends your content to users who watch workout videos, fitness reels, and health transformations. Relevance is not created through hashtags alone—it is created through consistent niche-specific content.

Performance refers to engagement during the first testing stage. When you post a Reel, Instagram shows it to a small sample of your followers and a handful of non-followers. It studies how they respond. If they pause instead of scroll, watch more than 50%, save it, share it, or follow you, the algorithm sees your content as promising. It then expands the reach. If engagement remains strong, your content enters multiple waves of distribution. The Explore page is often triggered during the second or third wave, when engagement exceeds average performance within your niche category. The more often your content hits these thresholds, the more frequently Instagram recommends your posts on Explore.

Audience behavior plays a larger role than most creators realize. The Explore page rewards creators whose followers consistently engage with their content. If your viewers like, save, share, or comment on your posts regularly, Instagram assumes your content is high-value. Conversely, if your followers rarely engage, the algorithm assumes your content is less relevant—even if your content is strong. This is why niche clarity and high-value content are essential. When your content speaks directly to your core audience, engagement becomes predictable. Predictability strengthens your recommendation score.

The Explore page also heavily relies on profile-level interest signals. This means Instagram doesn't recommend individual posts as much as it recommends creators who are consistently relevant within a category. Your page becomes categorized based on: your content topics, your follower demographics, your captions and keywords, your hashtag clusters, your on-screen text, and your engagement patterns. When these elements align, Instagram sees your page as "high-interest" for certain users. This leads to consistent placements on the Explore page over time—not just occasional spikes.

Another critical factor is your content structure. The Explore page favors content that generates high retention, strong emotional impact, and meaningful engagement. This means your Reels should ideally have strong hooks, smooth pacing, clear messaging, and impactful payoffs. Explore doesn't reward incomplete ideas or low clarity. It rewards content that makes people stay. Instagram's system tracks watch time very closely, especially the percentage of viewers who watch to the end. If a Reel has strong completion rates, it becomes a top candidate for Explore.

The Explore page also favors content that produces actions, not just views. Saves and shares carry significant weight. Comments also matter, especially if they are meaningful rather than generic. Follows, however, are a powerful indicator. When a high percentage of viewers who discover you on Explore end up following you, Instagram sees that as a strong recommendation signal. This means your content should clearly communicate your niche and value so new viewers know exactly why they should follow you.

Your visual branding and consistency also influence Explore performance. If your content maintains a recognizable visual style—whether through colors, text formatting, editing style, or tone—viewers are more likely to engage repeatedly. Repeated engagement trains the algorithm to identify you as a stable, predictable creator with a strong content identity. This makes your posts more attractive for recommendation.

Captions and keywords matter as well. Instagram reads your captions and matches them with user search behavior and interest patterns. If your captions include niche-specific keywords naturally, Instagram better understands what your posts are about. This helps your content appear on the Explore page for people searching for similar topics. Hashtags support this further by reinforcing your niche, but they are simply content categorization tools—not growth engines. The real power comes from aligning your niche with what your audience values most.

The Explore page favors creators who are consistent. When you post sporadically, your chances of hitting Explore decrease significantly because Instagram has less data to analyze. But when you post on a reliable schedule, the algorithm sees patterns that make it easier to predict performance. Predictability is the key to recommendation systems. The more predictable your engagement becomes, the more often you will appear on Explore.

What surprises most people is that Explore traffic often builds over time. A Reel may not appear on Explore the day it's posted. It may enter Explore a week later, after being tested with various groups. This is why deleting posts early is a mistake. Many Reels are slow burners. They gain traction gradually. When you understand wave distribution, you stop judging your content too quickly and allow the algorithm space to amplify your best ideas.

In summary, the Explore page is a powerful growth source for creators who combine niche clarity, high-value content, strong engagement patterns, and consistent posting. When you understand how Instagram identifies high recommendation posts, you stop relying on luck and start engineering your content for discovery. Once you crack the Explore code, your growth accelerates naturally, and you gain access to thousands of potential followers who are already interested in what you offer. Explore isn't random—it's strategic. And now, you know how to trigger it.

"The Day Her Content Hit Explore"

For as long as she could remember, Lila dreamed of growing her Instagram page into something meaningful—something that reached people, inspired them, and gave her a voice in her niche. But no matter how hard she tried, her content rarely reached beyond her own followers. She admired creators whose posts appeared on the Explore page, gaining thousands of views instantly. She wondered what made them special. Did they have better equipment? Better connections? Better luck? She didn't know that the Explore page wasn't magic—it was mathematics.

Lila spent months posting regularly, trying different ideas, testing different styles, and reading advice online. She used hashtags, studied trends, and experimented with time-of-day posting. But her reach still felt limited. Some Reels performed well, but others seemed to disappear without impact. She didn't realize that her niche was unclear, her messaging inconsistent, and her value unpredictable. The algorithm didn't know who to show her content to, and as a result, Explore didn't know where she belonged.

One night, she was scrolling through her analytics and noticed something that changed everything. Her best-performing videos all had something in common—they focused on a specific topic: simple productivity habits for overwhelmed creatives. These videos had higher saves, more shares, and deeper engagement. Her followers praised these videos the most. It clicked: she had stumbled onto her niche, but she had only posted about it occasionally. She decided to make a bold shift—she would dedicate her page to this niche fully.

The next week, she created a new Reel based on her niche. The hook was clear: "If you get overwhelmed easily, try this simple productivity shift." She kept the pacing tight, used on-screen text for clarity, and delivered a practical tip. She posted the video during her highest engagement window and logged off with cautious optimism.

A few hours later, she checked her phone and froze.

Her view count was surging—far beyond anything she had posted in months. Comments poured in. Saves spiked. People shared her video with friends. Her follower count began rising steadily. Something was different. Something was working. But she didn't yet realize what had happened.

The next day, she checked her insights and saw a number she had never seen before: **"Explore: 48,000 impressions."** Her heart raced. She had made it onto the Explore page. For the first time in her content creation journey, she had broken through the invisible wall. Instagram had recommended her content to thousands of non-followers.

But she didn't celebrate blindly. She studied the Reel carefully. She broke down every element—her niche clarity, her hook, the retention line, the crisp editing, the emotional connection, the practical value. She realized she had finally created content that aligned perfectly with what her audience wanted and what the algorithm supported. Encouraged, she repeated the process. New Reel, same niche, strong hook, emotional insight, practical takeaway. She posted again. This time, it reached even more non-followers. Within days, her Explore impressions multiplied. Her page grew faster than it ever had. Her confidence soared. She understood now that Explore wasn't about hoping—it was about engineering.

Weeks passed, and her page transformed. She became known in her niche. Her follower count doubled, then tripled. Opportunities she once only dreamed about became real. People messaged her daily. Her content mattered. Her voice mattered. It all began with one video that hit Explore and one decision to commit to her niche.

Lila's journey reflects a simple truth: the Explore page rewards clarity, value, and consistency. When she embraced her niche, the algorithm embraced her. When she created content that helped her audience genuinely, Explore recognized it. Her story proves that any creator—regardless of size—can unlock massive visibility when they align with what Instagram rewards.

That day on Explore didn't just change her analytics. It changed her identity. She no longer felt invisible. She felt seen. She felt understood. And she finally felt like she belonged.

Chapter 8

The Viral Trigger Framework: How to Structure Posts That Explode in Reach

Viral content may seem unpredictable, but in reality, viral posts follow a repeatable internal structure based on human psychology, audience identity, emotional resonance, and the patterns Instagram's algorithm recognizes as "high potential." When you understand how these elements interact, you can engineer content that has a significantly higher chance of going viral—not because of luck, but because your structure amplifies the triggers that spark rapid sharing, saving, and mass engagement. Viral content is not about replication; it is about alignment with the mind of the viewer. It is about meeting them where their attention already is and leading them through a predictable emotional arc that results in action.

The viral trigger framework includes five core elements: **tension**, **identity relevance**, **novelty**, **emotional resonance**, and **resolution**. When a post includes at least three of these elements, its chances of going viral increase dramatically. When all five are present, the content almost always enters multiple distribution waves. Understanding these elements allows you to reverse-engineer virality instead of hoping for it.

Tension is the first trigger. Viral videos almost always begin with tension—an unexpected statement, a bold claim, a strong emotion, a curiosity gap, or a challenge to the viewer's beliefs. Tension grabs attention because the brain is wired to resolve uncertainty. This is why hooks like "Most people do this wrong," "Here's what no one tells you," and "This might change your life" perform exceptionally well. Tension creates urgency. It creates suspense. And suspense increases retention. The longer the tension lasts, the more deeply the viewer invests in the content.

Identity relevance is the second trigger. Viral content speaks directly to who the viewer is—or who they want to become. Identity is the strongest motivator of engagement. When a video starts with "If you struggle with..." or "If you want to improve...," it taps into a viewer's sense of self. Identity relevance creates loyalty. It makes the viewer feel seen, understood, and represented. Viral posts are rarely general. They speak to a specific group in a specific way that resonates deeply. The narrower the identity targeting, the wider the spread within that group.

Novelty is the third trigger. The brain pays attention to what is new, surprising, innovative, or counterintuitive. Viral content often challenges conventional wisdom or introduces a fresh perspective. Novelty does not have to be groundbreaking—it just needs to feel different. Examples include surprising facts, unusual methods, unexpected tips, or unique angles. Novelty sparks curiosity. Curiosity increases watch time. And high watch time accelerates distribution. Novelty also makes content shareable because people love sharing ideas that make them feel informed or insightful.

Emotional resonance is the fourth trigger. Viral content makes people feel something—motivation, relief, hope, validation, joy, empowerment, nostalgia, or even discomfort. Emotion is the fuel behind shares. People share content that makes them feel understood or inspired because they want others to feel the same. Emotion increases saves because people want to revisit the feeling later. Emotion increases comments because they want to express their connection. Viral content is not sterile; it is human. It taps into universal emotions or deeply personal ones.

Resolution is the fifth trigger. Every viral post provides closure: a lesson, a transformation, a payoff, a truth, or a solution. Resolution completes the emotional arc. It gives the viewer a "takeaway." Viral Reels often end with a simple line:

"Do this," "Remember this," "Try this," "Save this," or "Share this." Strong resolution increases engagement depth. Without resolution, content may hook the viewer but fails to convert attention into action.

The viral trigger framework also includes structural principles. Viral videos almost always follow a smooth narrative flow: **hook → tension → value → emotional peak → resolution**. When this structure is executed well, retention naturally increases. This is why polished editing is not required. Messaging is what drives virality. Your message must evolve every few seconds, revealing new layers, insights, or emotions. If the message stalls, retention drops. Viral content feels like a fast-moving journey, not a static moment.

Another structural component is **accelerated pacing**. Viral videos move quickly—not chaotically, but purposefully. Every second introduces something new: a new phrase, visual, idea, or emotion. This creates momentum. Momentum keeps the viewer watching longer. Longer watch time is the algorithm's strongest signal that a post deserves widespread exposure.

Contrast is another viral accelerator. Before/after visuals, then/now comparisons, mistake/solution structures, or myth/fact formats perform exceptionally well. Contrast creates instant interest. It also makes retention more natural because the viewer wants to see the transformation complete. Humans crave completion. Viral videos give them a starting point and a finish point and keep them watching until the transition is revealed. **Relatability** is another crucial factor. Viral content often taps into shared experiences—stress, self-doubt, ambition, frustration, growth, discipline, health, beauty, money, productivity, or relationships. When viewers feel the content reflects their life, they engage deeply. Relatable content spreads because it connects people through universal truths.

The algorithm also looks at **engagement velocity**—how quickly a post receives interactions. Viral posts gain rapid early engagement because the content structure triggers immediate responses. Comments flood in because the content invites any form of expression. Saves rise because the message is powerful and repeatable. Shares spike because viewers want others to see it. High engagement velocity triggers large-scale distribution.

Another component of virality is **viewer identity validation**: the feeling of "This is so me." When content validates a viewer's internal beliefs, they engage. Viral creators understand this and produce content that supports, empowers, or challenges the viewer's internal narrative.

The final factor is **post purpose**. Viral posts have a clear purpose: to teach, inspire, transform, validate, reveal, or challenge. They are not random. They are intentional. Purpose creates resonance. Resonance creates spread.

By combining tension, identity relevance, novelty, emotional resonance, and resolution within a clear structure, you increase your chances of going viral dramatically. Virality is not random—it is engineered. When you understand the psychology behind it, you gain the ability to create content that spreads far beyond your followers and into the hearts, minds, and feeds of people around the world.

"The Post That Took Off Overnight"

Evan had been creating content for a long time, but nothing ever went viral. His posts got steady engagement, but they never exploded. He watched other creators grow rapidly while he felt stuck at the same level, wondering what secret they knew that he didn't. He tried different trends, music, topics, and editing styles, but nothing clicked. He believed virality was random—something that just happened if the algorithm chose you. That belief would change the night everything shifted.

One evening, Evan sat scrolling through Instagram, studying Reels that had millions of views. He noticed something he had never paid attention to before. Every viral Reel began with tension—something bold, emotional, or unexpected. He realized he had been starting his videos too gently, giving viewers no reason to stop scrolling. He wrote in his notes: "Start with tension."

Then he noticed something else. Viral videos spoke directly to a specific identity. "If you feel lost...," "If you struggle with confidence...," "If you're tired of starting over..." They weren't trying to reach everyone. They were targeting someone. He wrote again: "Speak to identity."

As he studied more videos, he recognized a pattern: each one had novelty—a surprising tip, truth, or angle he hadn't heard before. The content felt fresh. It sparked curiosity. He wrote: "Give them something unexpected."

He kept studying. Viral videos made him feel something—motivation, clarity, hope, or even discomfort. He realized he wasn't creating emotion; he was stating facts. He needed to connect with feelings. He wrote: "Trigger emotion."

Finally, he noticed every viral Reel had resolution. The message felt complete. He learned something. He gained something. The video left him with a takeaway. He wrote: "Offer resolution."

For the first time in his creator journey, Evan saw the blueprint.

That night, he crafted a new Reel using all five viral triggers. His hook said, "If you feel behind in life, listen to this." It created tension and identity relevance. In the body, he shared a surprising truth—that nobody is ahead or behind because life unfolds at different speeds. That was novelty and emotional resonance. He ended with a simple but powerful resolution: "Your journey is not late—it's uniquely yours." He added on-screen text. He kept the pacing smooth. He filmed it in one take.

He posted it without expectations and went to bed.

At 3 a.m., he woke up to hundreds of notifications.

His Reel had exploded.

Thousands of likes. Thousands of shares. Endless comments. People said they felt understood, seen, comforted, and inspired. The view count climbed rapidly every minute. He refreshed again and again, watching it surge.

By morning, the Reel had gone truly viral.

His follower count doubled overnight. Messages poured in. Other creators shared his video. People around the world stitched and remixed it. It spread far beyond his niche. It reached demographics he never targeted. It resonated across identities and experiences.

It wasn't luck.

It was structure.

Evan realized he had cracked the code—not because he posted more often, edited more creatively, or used a trending sound, but because he aligned his content with the psychological triggers that make people engage deeply. He finally understood virality wasn't magic—it was architecture. It was intention.

From that day forward, he created content differently. He led with tension. He spoke directly to identity. He added novelty. He infused emotion. He delivered resolution. His content didn't just perform—it impacted people. He grew faster, more consistently, and more powerfully than ever before.

The post that took off overnight didn't just change his analytics. It changed his belief. It made him realize that every creator has the potential to go viral—when they understand what truly makes people care.

Chapter 9

Consistency Without Burnout: Building a Sustainable Instagram Workflow That Lasts

One of the biggest challenges creators face on Instagram is staying consistent without burning out. Growth requires repeated momentum, but burnout destroys momentum completely. Most creators collapse not because they lack talent or ideas, but because they rely on inspiration rather than systems. They post when they feel motivated, disappear when they feel overwhelmed, and return only to repeat the cycle. But consistency is not about motivation. It is about structure. It is about building a workflow that supports you mentally, physically, and creatively. When your workflow is sustainable, you don't force yourself to create—you move naturally through a cycle that protects your energy while still delivering predictable content.

Burnout happens when creators focus too much on creation and not enough on organization. They film randomly, edit randomly, write captions randomly, and brainstorm randomly. This reactive workflow multiplies stress and makes Instagram feel like a burden. Sustainable consistency begins with one mindset shift: **You do not create content daily. You**

create systems that produce content daily. The difference between amateurs and professionals is not creativity—it is workflow. Professionals plan, batch, and organize. Amateurs try to do everything in real time.

The first step to a sustainable workflow is defining your content pillars. Once you know your niche, your pillars create a predictable structure for every week. You are no longer guessing what to post. You are rotating through established themes your audience already values. This removes 80% of the mental load of content creation. When your themes are aligned with your expertise and passion, brainstorming becomes effortless. Instead of waking up and wondering what to post, you select a pillar and generate ideas instantly.

The second step is batching. Batch creation is the most powerful tool for eliminating burnout. Batching means separating your workflow into stages—idea generation, scripting, filming, editing, captioning, and scheduling—rather than doing everything in one day. Trying to film, edit, and brainstorm daily is exhausting and inefficient. Your brain cannot switch between modes seamlessly. When you batch, your creativity stays focused. On idea days, you only brainstorm. On filming days, you focus only on filming. On editing days, you edit multiple videos at once. This significantly reduces your workload and protects your energy.

A sustainable batching cycle might look like this: one day of idea generation, one day of scripting, one day of filming, one day of editing, and one day of scheduling. You leave the remaining two days for engagement, rest, or additional content. This model produces three to five high-quality Reels per week with less stress and more clarity. Once you adopt this method, you realize consistency doesn't require endless effort—it requires smart sequencing.

The third step is simplifying your content style. The more complicated your videos are, the more friction you create for yourself. Viral videos are not complex—they are clear. They do not require perfect lighting, cinematic transitions, or advanced editing. They require strong messaging and structure. When you simplify your filming setup, your editing style, and your recording routine, you reduce the mental resistance that kills consistency. If filming takes too long, you won't film. If editing is stressful, you won't edit. Simplicity is the key to long-term success.

The fourth step is creating templates. Templates eliminate repetitive workload. You should have script templates, hook templates, caption templates, editing templates, and on-screen text templates. This saves hours every week and increases your productivity dramatically. Templates aren't rigid—they provide a starting point so you never begin from zero. When you have frameworks, creativity becomes faster and easier.

The fifth step is setting a content bank. A content bank is a collection of unused footage, scripts, ideas, drafts, and half-edited videos you can pull from anytime. This protects you when life gets busy. A content bank ensures that even when you're stressed, tired, or uninspired, you can still maintain your posting rhythm. Consistency is not about endless creativity—it is about resourcefulness.

The sixth step is managing your energy, not just your time. Some creators are most creative in the morning; others in the evening. Some prefer long filming sessions; others prefer short bursts. Your workflow must match your personal energy patterns. Trying to create when your brain is tired only leads to burnout. Your best content comes when you honor your energy instead of fighting it. When you align your schedule with your natural rhythms, consistency becomes sustainable.

The seventh step is protecting your mental health by avoiding unnecessary metrics. Obsession with likes, views, and comments creates emotional fatigue. It distracts you from your process. Sustainable creators focus on improving their content, not on obsessing over analytics. Metrics are useful for evaluation, but they should not control your emotions. When you measure improvement instead of performance, burnout decreases dramatically.

The eighth step is practicing micro-consistency instead of macro-consistency. Macro-consistency means posting every single day without fail. Micro-consistency means committing to small, achievable actions that build momentum. Even on tough days, you can brainstorm one idea, script one hook, or edit one clip. Micro-consistency allows you to move forward even when life gets heavy. Small progress maintains momentum without overwhelming you.

The ninth step is building rest into your workflow. Rest is not a reward. Rest is part of the strategy. Creativity comes from clarity, not exhaustion. When you schedule rest intentionally, you prevent burnout before it begins. You become more inspired, more focused, and more productive. Rest is a competitive advantage. Burnout is a growth killer.

The final step is accepting that consistency does not mean perfection. You will miss days. You will have slow weeks. You will have moments where inspiration fades. Sustainable creators do not quit during these moments—they adjust. They return to their systems. They rebuild momentum gradually. They trust the compound effect. Consistency is not about never falling. It is about always getting back up with intention.

When you master consistency without burnout, Instagram

stops feeling overwhelming. It becomes a structured part of your life rather than a stressful demand. You no longer fear posting. You no longer feel guilty for resting. You no longer question whether you are doing enough. You move with clarity, confidence, and purpose. And most importantly, your growth becomes stable, predictable, and long-lasting.

"The Week She Finally Stopped Burning Out"

For months, Sofia pushed herself to post constantly on Instagram. Every day she filmed something new, edited late into the night, and forced herself to brainstorm ideas even when she was exhausted. At first, her momentum felt exciting. She got a few viral videos, grew some followers, and felt hopeful. But over time, her energy faded. The pressure to create daily content slowly drained her. She began dreading the camera. Her ideas stalled. Her motivation collapsed. What once felt fun now felt suffocating. Sofia didn't realize she wasn't failing—her system was failing.

One afternoon, overwhelmed and defeated, she opened her camera roll and saw hundreds of unfinished videos, chaotic clips, half-written scripts, and abandoned ideas. She realized she wasn't lacking content—she was lacking structure. She felt like she was running on a treadmill that never stopped. Every day she started from zero, trying to film, edit, brainstorm, and post all at the same time. The workload was unsustainable. She understood in that moment she couldn't keep going this way.

The next day, she came across a creator she admired who shared her workflow. It was simple, structured, and shockingly different from Sofia's approach. Instead of creating daily, this creator batched her content. She filmed once a week, edited once a week, brainstormed once a week, and posted according to a plan. She looked calm, organized, and energized—everything Sofia was not. Sofia felt a wave of relief wash over her. Maybe consistency didn't require chaos. Maybe there was a better way.

Inspired, she redesigned her entire process. She chose her niche clearly and defined four content pillars. Instantly, brainstorming became easier. She didn't need to invent ideas—she simply needed to rotate through her pillars. She set aside one day for brainstorming, one for scripting, one for filming, and one for editing. She treated her workflow like a cycle, not a sprint.

When filming day came, she was nervous but prepared. She filmed five Reels in under two hours—something that used to take her days. She felt empowered. She felt efficient. She felt in control for the first time in months. Editing day was lighter because she wasn't worried about brainstorming. Scheduling day felt peaceful because all the hard work was already done. She realized she had been suffocating herself with unnecessary pressure. She didn't need to be "always on." She needed a system.

As weeks passed, Sofia noticed a dramatic change. She no longer dreaded posting. She felt creative again. She started enjoying filming, writing, and interacting with her audience. Her engagement improved because she was more consistent and more energized. She had time to think, reflect, rest, and reconnect with her purpose. Slowly, she built a content bank filled with unused videos, drafts, and scripts. She never ran out of ideas anymore. She felt safe, prepared, and confident.

Her biggest breakthrough came during a chaotic week when everything went wrong—family emergencies, work stress, exhaustion. In the past, she would have disappeared from Instagram completely. But thanks to her content bank, she had three fully edited Reels ready to post. She didn't break her consistency. Her audience didn't notice her difficult week. Instagram continued rewarding her regular engagement. For the first time, she realized how powerful a sustainable workflow truly was.

The week she finally stopped burning out was the week she took control of her creativity again. She learned that consistency is not about pushing harder—it's about designing smarter. It's about honoring your energy. It's about respecting your mental health. It's about creating systems that carry you when life gets heavy. Sofia's journey proved that once you eliminate burnout, your true creative power finally emerges.

Chapter 10

Turning Followers into Fans: Building Community, Trust, and Long-Term Engagement

Growing an Instagram account is one thing. Turning those followers into fans—people who trust you, return to you, and engage with you consistently—is another level entirely. Followers alone do not create impact, income, or opportunity. Fans do. Fans are the people who save your posts, share your insights, comment deeply, watch your videos to the end, buy your products, join your programs, and support your long-term vision. Fans feel connected to you because you've created a relationship, not just content. This chapter will show you how to transform casual followers into loyal community members who view you as a meaningful part of their daily life.

The foundation of building fans is **trust**. Trust is created through consistency, clarity, authenticity, and value. When a creator posts unpredictable content, followers lose clarity. When a creator disappears frequently, followers lose confidence. When a creator lacks intention, followers lose interest. But when your content is consistent in topic, tone, message, and frequency, your audience begins to trust your reliability. They know what to expect from you. They begin to see you as a stable voice in a noisy world. Stability creates trust. Trust creates fans.

The next element is **connection**. People follow information, but they stay for connection. Connection is built through storytelling, relatability, vulnerability, and presence. When you share struggles, insights, lessons, or personal breakthroughs, you allow your audience to see themselves in your journey. When you show that you understand their struggles, you build emotional bonds. Fans don't love you because you're perfect—they love you because you're human and helpful. This emotional connection is the bridge that turns spectators into supporters.

Engagement depth is also essential. Shallow engagement happens when a viewer likes a post and leaves. Deep engagement happens when they comment thoughtfully, send your content to friends, reply to your Stories, or DM you with questions. To nurture deep engagement, you must invite it. Ask questions. Encourage conversation. Use Story polls, question boxes, and "comment prompts" to spark interaction. Instagram's algorithm rewards creators who produce deep engagement, and deep engagement strengthens community bonds.

Community-building also requires **reciprocity**—the willingness to engage with your audience in return. Responding to comments, liking replies, acknowledging DMs, and interacting with your followers' content can dramatically increase loyalty. People engage more when they feel seen. When followers know you are present, responsive, and appreciative, they develop a sense of belonging. Belonging is a powerful driver of long-term engagement.

Another key factor in turning followers into fans is **identity alignment**. Fans see your content as part of who they are or who they want to become. When your message aligns with their identity or their desired identity, they attach emotionally to your brand. For example, a creator who consistently posts fitness content becomes part of a follower's "fitness identity." A financial creator becomes part of their "wealth-building identity." A motivational creator becomes part of their "self-growth identity." Identity alignment transforms content from entertainment into lifestyle influence.

To build fans, you must also offer **predictable value**. Predictable value means your followers know what they will gain from your page every time they see your content. Whether it's motivation, education, humor, inspiration, or transformation, your value must be consistent. Fans crave reliability. They want to know they can count on you. When your value is predictable, your brand becomes part of their routine. Community loyalty is strengthened when you share **micro-stories**—small insights from your daily life, behind-the-scenes moments, personal wins, challenges, and lessons. These stories make you relatable. They show your humanity. They allow followers to feel close to you even if they've never met you. Micro-stories turn creators into companions, and companions become trusted voices.

Another powerful strategy is creating **signature content**—unique formats, phrases, angles, or storytelling styles that people associate specifically with you. Signature content builds brand recall. It creates familiarity. It makes your content instantly recognizable. Fans love recognition. When they see your signature elements, they feel at home.

To convert followers into fans, you must also create **safe spaces**. This can be your DMs, your comments section, your Stories, or even a dedicated community group. Safe spaces allow people to express themselves, ask questions, and feel supported. When followers feel safe, they trust you more. Trust becomes loyalty. Loyalty becomes advocacy.

Finally, turning followers into fans requires consistency—not just in posting, but in **presence**. Fans need to feel like you show up for them. This doesn't mean living on Instagram. It means showing genuine care. It means being reliable. It means offering value even when no one is watching. When you maintain presence, your influence compounds.

To build a community that lasts, you must think long-term. Slow, steady relationship-building always outperforms quick engagement hacks. Fans are built over time through repeated moments of value, connection, and authenticity. When you master these principles, you develop a community that not only watches your content but believes in your message, supports your mission, and grows with you.

"The Moment Her Followers Became a Family"

For months, Clara had been growing her Instagram page steadily. Her Reels performed well. Her follower count increased. Her content was consistent. Yet something felt missing. Despite her numbers rising, her audience felt distant—silent, passive, disconnected. People watched her videos but didn't interact deeply. They liked her content but didn't seem invested in her. She wanted more than numbers. She wanted impact. She wanted community. She wanted to feel like she was helping real people, not chasing empty metrics.

One evening, after posting another polished Reel, she noticed her comments section was almost empty. She felt frustrated.

She wanted connection, not just views. On impulse, she posted a Story sharing a personal struggle she'd been facing—nothing dramatic, just honest. She talked about self-doubt, exhaustion, and the pressure to always be strong. She didn't expect a response.

Within minutes, her inbox filled with messages.

People thanked her for sharing. People told her they felt the same. People appreciated her vulnerability. It was the most engagement she had received in months. She realized something powerful: people didn't need perfection—they needed honesty. They needed connection. They needed to see the human behind the camera.

The next day, Clara posted a Reel that was different from her usual style. Instead of teaching, she told a story—her story. She spoke directly to the viewer, not as an expert, but as a friend. The response was overwhelming. Comments flooded in. People related. People shared their experiences. People expressed gratitude. Something had shifted. Her audience felt seen, and in return, they saw her.

Over the following weeks, Clara focused intentionally on building deeper connections. She responded to comments daily. She asked questions in her captions. She used polls and Q&A boxes in her Stories. She shared behind-the-scenes clips and simple moments from her life. She supported her followers just as they supported her. Gradually, her page began to feel alive—warm, engaged, familiar.

Her biggest breakthrough came when she launched a weekly interactive series where she answered follower questions live. She didn't know what to expect, but hundreds showed up. They listened. They laughed. They supported each other. They supported her. For the first time, Clara realized she wasn't just building an audience—she was building a family.

One night, she received a long message from a follower who said her content had helped them overcome a difficult chapter. They wrote that her words made them feel less alone. Clara sat in silence for a moment, overwhelmed with emotion. She understood then that this was the true purpose of her platform. Not views. Not numbers. Connection. Impact. Community. Her followers were no longer strangers—they were people she served, supported, and inspired.

As her community grew stronger, everything changed. Her engagement doubled. Her retention increased. Her content spread further. But what mattered most was the feeling—her audience trusted her, and she trusted them. She no longer felt like she was speaking into a void. She felt like she was speaking to real people who cared, who listened, who grew with her.

The moment her followers became a family was the moment her entire creator journey transformed. Clara learned that fans are created through kindness, authenticity, and presence—not perfection. Her story is a reminder that real influence comes not from how many people watch you, but from how deeply they connect with you.

Chapter 11

Analytics That Matter: Understanding What to Track and What to Ignore

One of the biggest mistakes creators make on Instagram is obsessing over the wrong analytics. They watch likes, view counts, and follower numbers with emotional urgency, believing these metrics determine their success. But the truth is that the most commonly monitored metrics are often the least important. Likes do not tell you whether your content created value. Follower count does not tell you whether you're building a loyal community. View count does not tell you whether your message resonated. If you focus too much on vanity metrics, you ignore the data that actually drives growth. Real growth comes from understanding how to read the right numbers and use them to improve your content strategy over time.

The first step in mastering Instagram analytics is shifting your mindset from emotional interpretation to strategic interpretation. Analytics are not a judgment—they are information. They tell you what works, what doesn't, what your audience values, and what the algorithm recognizes as high-performing content. When you learn to read analytics unemotionally, you gain control. You stop panicking over low-performing posts and start understanding why they underperformed. You stop relying on guesswork and start making data-backed decisions. You stop creating blindly and start creating intentionally.

The most important metric on Instagram is **retention rate**. Retention tells you how long viewers watched your video before scrolling away. If people leave early, your hook or pacing is weak. If they stay until the end, your messaging is strong. High retention signals to Instagram that your content is engaging, which increases distribution. Retention matters more than likes, comments, or view count because it measures attention—the currency of social media. If your retention is weak, your reach will always be limited. If your retention is strong, your content will consistently enter new recommendation waves.

The second most important metric is **rewatch rate**—the percentage of viewers who watch your Reel more than once. Rewatches tell the algorithm that your content has high value, either due to clarity, inspiration, emotional connection, or practical steps. Rewatching is a powerful psychological signal. It means the viewer wants to process the information again or experience the feeling again. Rewatch rate is also closely tied to virality because videos that people watch multiple times tend to accumulate more saves and shares.

The third critical metric is **engagement depth**, not just engagement number. Engagement depth includes saves, shares, and meaningful comments. Saves indicate long-term value. Shares indicate emotional or educational impact. Comments—especially thoughtful ones—indicate connection. Engagement depth tells Instagram your content is worth recommending widely. Shallow metrics like likes do not offer meaningful insight. Deep engagement shows that your content resonates strongly.

Another important metric is **follower conversion rate**—how many viewers follow you after watching your Reel. This metric shows whether your content communicates your niche, your identity, and your value clearly. If people enjoy your video but don't follow you, your message may be unclear or your niche may be too broad. If your conversion rate is high, your content aligns well with your ideal audience. Follower conversion is a key measure of long-term growth potential.

You must also analyze **completion rate**, the percentage of viewers who watch your video from beginning to end. Completion rate is directly tied to retention. A high completion rate tells Instagram your Reel holds attention effectively. A low completion rate signals weak structure, unclear messaging, or poor pacing. Completion rate is often the difference between a

Reel reaching thousands or tens of thousands. It is one of the algorithm's primary ranking factors.

Another overlooked metric is **average watch time**. Even if viewers don't watch the full video, strong average watch time indicates your content held attention longer than the average Reel in your category. The algorithm compares your watch time to similar content from other creators. If you outperform your category, your content gets promoted. If you underperform, your distribution weakens. Understanding how watch time fluctuates with different hooks, pacing styles, and topics allows you to refine your content more intelligently.

Creators often obsess over **view counts**, but view counts alone are misleading. A video might get many views but low retention, which means the algorithm tested it widely but it didn't perform well. Another video may receive fewer views but strong retention and high engagement depth, which means it is far more valuable for long-term growth. Instead of chasing high view counts, you should chase strong ratios—high saves per view, high shares per view, high watch time per second. Ratios predict growth. Views alone do not.

Another common misconception is that low-performing posts should be deleted. In reality, deleting posts hurts your understanding of your audience. Low-performing content provides clarity. It shows you what not to repeat. It reveals which hooks fail, which topics lose interest, which editing styles weaken retention, and which messages do not resonate. Every low-performing post is data—not failure. Leaving posts up also maintains the stability of your account's content library, which the algorithm uses to categorize your niche.

Analyzing post timing is also essential. Compare your performance across different time windows to identify patterns in your audience's behavior. Look for trends in engagement peaks. Study how weekend posts perform differently from weekday posts. Notice when your content receives its first distribution wave and when it enters subsequent waves. Timing is not a guess—it is a pattern.

Another metric to track is **audience demographics**. Understanding age, location, peak activity hours, and gender distribution helps you refine your messaging, hooks, and content style. If your audience skews younger, fast-paced and visually dynamic content performs better. If your audience skews older, educational and intentional content performs better. Demographics guide your strategy.

Lastly, you must track **topic performance**. Study which topics consistently generate engagement and which ones fall flat. Often, your audience tells you what they want through their behavior. When you align your content with top-performing themes, your growth accelerates naturally.

By focusing on retention, rewatch rate, engagement depth, conversion rate, completion rate, and audience behavior, you gain clarity. You gain direction. You stop guessing. Analytics become your compass, not your burden. When you track the right data, you build the right strategy. And when your strategy aligns with your analytics, your growth becomes consistent, predictable, and scalable.

"The Numbers That Changed His Strategy Forever"

Elias had been creating content for a long time, but his growth felt inconsistent. Some videos performed well, others flopped, and he could never pinpoint why. Whenever a post underperformed, he took it personally. Whenever a post went viral, he thought it was luck. He checked his likes obsessively. He tracked his follower count daily. His emotions rose and fell with the numbers. But none of the numbers he focused on actually helped him grow. He didn't yet understand which metrics mattered or how to interpret them.

One night, feeling discouraged after a low-performing Reel, Elias opened his analytics out of frustration. Instead of fixating on likes, he clicked deeper into the data—something he rarely did. What he saw surprised him. His retention curve showed viewers dropping off within the first two seconds. His hook wasn't working. On another video, his retention was high but his follower conversion was low. People liked the content, but it didn't reflect his niche clearly enough. On another post, his average watch time was excellent, but his saves were low. He realized the content was interesting but not actionable.

For the first time, Elias saw clues instead of disappointments.

He spent an hour analyzing his data thoroughly, and patterns emerged. The videos with the highest retention all had strong hooks. The ones with the most saves offered clear steps. The ones with the most shares triggered emotion. The ones with the highest conversion rates spoke directly to his niche. Suddenly, analytics were no longer numbers—they were insights. They were a language he hadn't learned yet.

The next day, Elias created a Reel designed intentionally with his data in mind. He crafted a concise hook. He emphasized clarity. He added on-screen steps to increase saveability. He ended with a takeaway to encourage shares. He posted it during a time when his analytics showed his audience was most active. Within hours, the video gained strong retention and entered a second distribution wave. It didn't go viral, but it performed significantly better than his recent posts. More importantly, it performed exactly as his analytics predicted.

Encouraged, Elias began analyzing every post like a scientist. He studied his retention curves, tested new hooks, experimented with pacing, and refined his topics. His content became sharper and more aligned with his audience's needs. His engagement deepened. His growth stabilized. The emotional rollercoaster he once rode began to fade. He no longer took low-performing posts personally. He took them analytically. Every "failure" became data. Every success became a blueprint.

His breakthrough came a month later, when a Reel he created specifically to maximize retention and emotional resonance went viral. The retention curve stayed high. The rewatch rate spiked. Saves exploded. Shares multiplied. His analytics predicted its success before it even took off. This time, he didn't feel shocked. He felt empowered.

For the first time in his creator journey, Elias understood that growth wasn't luck. It was logic. It was structure. It was data. The numbers that once discouraged him now guided him. He learned that when you track the right metrics, you gain clarity. When you gain clarity, you gain control. And when you gain control, you gain momentum.

The numbers changed his strategy forever. They transformed him from a guessing creator into an intentional one. They lifted the weight of emotional pressure and replaced it with confidence. Elias no longer feared analytics—he relied on them. He finally understood what his audience valued, how the algorithm interpreted his content, and what he needed to adjust to grow consistently.

His story is a reminder that knowledge is power, and the right numbers give you that power. When you stop chasing vanity metrics and start understanding meaningful analytics, your content improves, your confidence grows, and your Instagram journey becomes a path you can navigate with certainty instead of guesswork.

Chapter 12

The Long-Term Growth Blueprint: Building an Instagram Strategy That Compounds for Years

Short-term growth feels exciting, but long-term growth is where creators build careers, opportunities, and sustainable influence. Many creators experience temporary spikes—viral moments, sudden bursts of followers, or waves of engagement. But only a small percentage maintain momentum over months and years. The difference between temporary creators and long-term creators is strategy. Long-term growth is not accidental. It is intentional, structured, and aligned with principles that compound over time. A long-term Instagram strategy isn't about trying to go viral every day. It's about creating a system that allows your reach, reputation, and influence to expand steadily month after month.

The foundation of long-term growth is **niche mastery**. When your niche is clear, your message becomes consistent. When your message is consistent, your audience grows predictably. When your audience grows predictably, your brand strengthens. Long-term success is not built on randomness or jumping between topics constantly. It is built on becoming a trusted voice in a focused area. Mastering one niche creates a stable base that supports expansion later. When your audience trusts you within a specific niche, they follow you consistently and engage deeply.

The second pillar of long-term growth is **content evolution**. The creators who last are not the ones who repeat the same format forever—they evolve. Instagram changes, trends shift, and audience interests evolve, yet the core principles of value remain. Long-term creators study what their audience responds to and adjust accordingly. They refine their hooks, improve their pacing, deepen their messaging, take creative risks, and adapt to new formats without abandoning their core identity. Evolution keeps your content fresh, your audience engaged, and your brand relevant.

Another essential pillar of long-term growth is **relationship building**. Creators who build genuine relationships with their audience retain attention far longer than those who focus solely on reach. Long-term success depends on connection, trust, and community. This includes responding to comments, speaking to your audience directly, sharing personal stories, asking questions, and making your followers feel valued. Community-driven creators grow consistently because their audience doesn't just like their content—they like *them*. Relationships create loyalty, and loyalty sustains growth long-term. The fourth pillar is **consistent posting cycles**.

Long-term growth requires predictable, manageable consistency. Not daily pressure, but structured rhythm. Three to five high-quality Reels per week over years will outperform brief bursts of daily posting followed by burnout. Long-term creators understand the power of sustainability. They use batching, templates, content banks, and simple editing workflows to maintain consistency without sacrificing their well-being. Consistency is the engine of long-term growth. Without consistency, momentum disappears.

The fifth pillar is **skills improvement**. The creators who last are the ones who constantly upgrade their craft—hook writing, storytelling, editing, teaching, on-camera confidence, and audience understanding. Long-term success requires mastery. Mastery is built through repetition, experimentation, and learning. When you improve your skills week by week, your content quality increases naturally, your retention rises, and your audience grows steadily. Skills compound the same way money does. Small improvements accumulate into massive results over time.

The sixth pillar is **leveraging trends strategically**. Long-term creators don't rely on trends, but they use trends intelligently. Trends are accelerators, not foundations. A trend can boost reach temporarily, but it cannot replace consistent value. When combined with strong messaging, trends can expose your content to thousands of new people who later become long-term followers. But trends must align with your niche and your audience; otherwise, the reach will be meaningless. Strategic trend use accelerates long-term growth without destabilizing your brand.

The seventh pillar is **data-driven decisions**. Long-term creators don't guess what works—they measure what works. They study retention curves, rewatch rates, saves, shares, and follower conversion. They track which hooks perform best and which topics resonate most. They refine their strategy based on data, not emotion. Data reveals what your audience values. When you follow the data, your long-term trajectory becomes predictable.

The eighth pillar is **diversifying content formats**. While Reels are currently the fastest growth engine, long-term creators use a mix of content forms—Reels for reach, Stories for connection, carousels for education, and Lives for depth. This diversification strengthens retention and builds multiple layers of engagement. It also protects you from algorithm shifts. When you diversify your content, your page becomes a multi-dimensional brand instead of a one-format creator.

The ninth pillar is **brand building**. Long-term growth requires building a recognizable brand—visual style, messaging style, tone, signature elements, and a consistent voice. Your brand becomes the glue that binds your content together. It makes you memorable, shareable, and trustworthy. When people recognize your content instantly, your influence multiplies. Branding is not about aesthetics—it is about identity. A clear brand identity becomes your long-term competitive advantage.

The tenth pillar is **monetization alignment**. Long-term creators design their content with monetization in mind—not in a salesy way, but in a strategic way. When your content is aligned with your long-term business goals, each post becomes a stepping stone toward income. Monetization gives you stability, which allows you to create consistently for years. Whether you sell digital products, UGC packages, affiliate offers, memberships, or coaching, monetization is what transforms long-term growth into a sustainable creator career.

The final pillar of long-term growth is **patience**. Long-term creators understand that mastery takes time, audiences grow slowly, relationships deepen over months, and momentum compounds gradually. They do not quit after slow weeks or difficult months. They do not let fluctuations discourage them. They trust the process. They trust their systems. They trust the compound effect of consistent effort. Patience is the most underrated skill in the creator journey, but it is the one that determines whether you will still be creating successfully years from now.

Long-term growth is not about working harder—it is about working smarter, with structure, intention, and clarity. When you follow this blueprint, your growth becomes not just possible, but inevitable. The compound effect of consistent, strategic effort creates results far greater than any single viral moment ever could.

"The Year Her Strategy Finally Compounded"

When Ava first started creating content, she focused entirely on going viral. Every video she made was designed to explode. She chased trends obsessively, copied top creators, and posted daily with high intensity. At first, her strategy worked—she got a few viral videos, her follower count jumped, and she felt unstoppable. But after a few months, her reach slowed. Her engagement dipped. She felt confused. Why wasn't she sustaining the growth she had worked so hard for? She didn't realize her strategy was built on sparks, not foundations.

One evening, after a disappointing week, Ava sat down to review her content. She realized she had no niche. She talked about fitness one day, productivity the next, mindset the next, and beauty the next. Her audience didn't know what she stood for. She had been chasing visibility rather than building identity. It hit her—she wasn't building a brand. She was posting for quick hits. And quick hits burn out fast.

The next day, she made a decision: she would rebuild her strategy from the ground up. She chose one niche she was deeply passionate about—simplifying wellness for busy women. Suddenly, everything felt clearer. Her topics aligned. Her messaging aligned. Her ideas flowed naturally. Her audience responded immediately. She felt focused for the first time in months.

As she continued, Ava evolved her content gradually. She studied retention, rewrote hooks, improved her storytelling, and simplified her filming style. She practiced her on-camera presence. She refined her aesthetic. She learned from every post. Little by little, her content became smoother, sharper, more impactful. Not because she worked harder, but because she improved her skills intentionally.

She also began nurturing her audience more deeply. She replied to comments, asked questions, created polls, shared personal stories, and created space for her followers to feel seen. Her engagement deepened. Her followers became invested. She no longer had spectators—she had a community. And community members don't disappear when the algorithm shifts. Ava built systems. She batched her filming. She created templates. She stored extra content in a bank. She developed a consistent weekly cycle. She stopped relying on motivation. She relied on structure. Her stress decreased. Her creativity increased. What once felt frantic now felt organized, sustainable, and enjoyable.

The turning point came eight months later. She reviewed her analytics and saw something she had never seen before—every month had grown slightly more than the last. Not explosively, not dramatically, but steadily, predictably, and consistently. Her views were trending upward. Her saves were increasing. Her shares were multiplying. Her follower count wasn't spiking—it was compounding. She realized she had built something rare: momentum that didn't rely on virality.

One afternoon, she posted a Reel that represented everything she had learned throughout the year—clean messaging, clear value, emotional resonance, and a strong hook. The video didn't go viral instantly. But within two weeks, it entered multiple waves of recommendation, reached hundreds of thousands of people, and brought in thousands of new followers. It didn't explode overnight—but it grew steadily, just like she had grown steadily.

Ava no longer cared about temporary spikes. She cared about long-term stability. She understood that real success came from consistent value, not random luck. Her brand had a voice. Her audience trusted her. Her content held meaning. She finally felt like a real creator.

By the end of the year, Ava looked back on her journey and realized the power of compounding. Every small improvement, every consistent post, every engagement, every adjustment, every learning moment had built upon the last. She wasn't growing because of one moment—she was growing because of hundreds of intentional moments stacked together.

Her story is a reminder that the long-term blueprint doesn't reward impatience—it rewards resilience, clarity, and consistency. The year her strategy finally compounded was the same year she discovered what true growth actually feels like: steady, fulfilling, and unstoppable.

Epilogue

The Creator Who Decided to Grow With Intention

The journey through Instagram growth is often portrayed as a glamorous whirlwind of viral moments, sudden success, and massive followings. But the truth is far more grounded and far more empowering. Real growth comes from decisions—small, consistent, intentional decisions that compound over time. If you've reached the end of this book, you've already taken the first and most important step: choosing to create with purpose. Choosing to grow with intention. Choosing to understand the platform rather than fear it. Choosing strategy over guessing, clarity over confusion, and sustainability over burnout. This decision alone separates you from the countless creators who quit long before their potential ever takes form.

You now understand what most creators never learn. You understand that growth isn't about luck—it's about structure. It's about building systems rather than relying on motivation. It's about mastering the fundamentals: hooks, retention, value, timing, niche, storytelling, and consistency. These are not tricks. These are not trends. These are not passing hacks. These are timeless principles rooted in human psychology and platform behavior. Once you understand them, you are no longer at the mercy of the algorithm—you are aligned with it.

You play the game with clarity instead of confusion. You create from a position of strength rather than insecurity.

As you move forward, your journey will unfold in phases. Some seasons will bring rapid growth. Some will feel slow. Some videos will explode. Others will quietly gather dust. But none of it is wasted. Every phase teaches you something. In seasons of growth, you learn what resonates. In seasons of plateau, you refine your strategy. In seasons of slowdown, you deepen your understanding. And in seasons of breakthrough, you experience the reward of everything you have built. The creator journey is not linear—it is cyclical. The creators who learn, adapt, and endure through these cycles are the ones who build legacies.

There will be days when the algorithm feels unpredictable or unfair. Days when a video you love underperforms. Days when you question your direction or compare yourself to others. These moments don't mean you're failing—they mean you're human. Every successful creator has faced them. What separates the ones who succeed from the ones who quit is their ability to return to their fundamentals. When you refine your hooks, your clarity returns. When you stick to your niche, your audience strengthens. When you focus on value, your content improves. When you track meaningful analytics, your decisions sharpen. You now have everything you need to navigate those moments with confidence.

In this digital era, Instagram is more than a platform. It is a stage. A voice. A global connection point. A modern portfolio. A business. A creative canvas. A personal brand. And most importantly, a pathway to opportunity. Whether your goal is to monetize, inspire, educate, entertain, or build community, the foundation remains the same: understand the psychology of your audience and the mechanics of the platform. When you align both, growth becomes a natural byproduct. You no longer chase the algorithm—the algorithm amplifies what you already do well.

As you continue building, remember that momentum is created through repetition. Not perfection. Not virality. Not pressure. Momentum is built by showing up repeatedly, refining your craft, learning from each post, and treating every piece of content as data, feedback, and progress. Over time, these repetitions create mastery. Mastery creates impact. And impact creates influence that lasts far beyond any single post.

Your creator journey will not be identical to anyone else's—and it shouldn't be. Your voice, your story, your perspective, and your mission are uniquely yours. This is the greatest advantage you possess. Lean into it. Refine it. Protect it. Your individuality is the magnet that attracts your true audience. The more you embrace your identity as a creator, the more magnetic your content becomes.

Now you stand at the beginning of the real journey—the implementation. You have the blueprint. You have the frameworks. You have the strategy. You have the understanding. The only remaining step is action. You do not need to feel ready. You need only to begin. Begin with the next idea. The next piece of content. The next batch day. The next thoughtful adjustment. Growth comes from movement, and movement creates transformation.

The creator who succeeds is not the one with the most talent. It is the one with the most resilience, clarity, and intention. You now hold all three. As long as you continue creating, learning, and refining, your growth is inevitable. Your influence is inevitable. Your success is inevitable. You did not reach the end of this book by accident—you reached it because you decided to build something meaningful.

And now, you are ready to grow not just an account, but an ecosystem. Not just followers, but fans. Not just reach, but resonance. Not just content, but legacy. Your Instagram journey from this point forward is no longer reactive—it is strategic. No longer overwhelming—it is structured. No longer uncertain—it is intentional. This is the beginning of your long-term growth story. And the chapters ahead will be written by the creator you are becoming—powerful, consistent, and unstoppable.

www.ingramcontent.com/pod-product-compliance
Lightning Source LLC
LaVergne TN
LVHW022230200926
848481LV00006B/2198